A GOLDEN LEGACY

A GOLDEN LEGACY tells the story of a man whose impact deserves to be remembered. Sam's presence has been both monumental and historic, shaping not only the OCC but also the broader banking community. More importantly, he dedicated himself to the growth of others, serving as a trusted leader, mentor, and friend to countless individuals. Ultimately, readers will come to see that Sam Golden stands as a true giant among men, leaving an enduring legacy of influence and inspiration.

Vernon Stafford Jr
CEO, LeviaTrust Consulting

A GOLDEN LEGACY BEAUTIFULLY captures the sterling character and inspiring spirit of Sam Golden, from the very first page to the final words. Although he faced his share of challenges, Sam has met each one with grace and remarkable success. This book is certain to inspire others to persevere with the same strength and dignity.

Jack H. Moore
Director, Gulf Coast Medical Foundation

GROUNDED IN HIS FAITH, family and commitment to serving others, Sam Golden's legacy is truly Golden. *A Golden Legacy* reflects the love, kindness, and unwavering optimism that radiate from him. Reading this book will leave a lasting impression and inspire the readers to "raise their game" in living a values-centered life. Without question, it captures the essence of Sam and the remarkable people and experiences that shaped him into the extraordinary man he is today.

Cathy Bryce
UNT System Board of Regents

FROM THE VERY FIRST pages of Sam's memoir, readers gain a true sense of what a remarkable man he is. His story is one of love, determination, and devotion – where he began, how he persevered, and the people who have walked beside him will inspire all who read it. Having served as his leadership and executive coach, I can say with certainty why Sam was, and continues to be, an extraordinary leader. A Golden Legacy is the blueprint for other leaders to follow the model Sam has set.

Jo Ann Lucero

Leadership and Executive Coach, "Cultivating Thinking Partnerships"

I HAD THE PRIVILEGE of working alongside Sam Golden for many years, and reading A Golden Legacy brought back vivid memories of those times. Working shoulder to shoulder with Sam was a masterclass in integrity and grace under pressure, and this book perfectly reflects the principled, uplifting leader we knew in the office. His example has the power to change the way you approach both work and life, and readers will come away inspired by the lessons he lived every day.

Mark A. Nishan

Former OCC Chief of Staff

A GOLDEN LEGACY reveals the exceptional character of my friend, Sam Golden. He is a man of strong faith, devoted to his family and consistently lives out the spirit of a Good Samaritan. As his memoir reflects, Sam has faced life's challenges with resilience, turning obstacles into accomplishments and lasting success. Readers, especially younger generations, will find inspiration in his journey and be motivated to pursue lives of purpose, integrity, and service.

Charles Cone

Treasured & "Golden" Friend

A GOLDEN LEGACY

FAITH, FAMILY AND A LIFE OF PURPOSE

A MEMOIR

SAMUEL P. GOLDEN
with Angie Ransome-Jones

A Golden Legacy
Faith, Family and a Life of Purpose

Hardcover ISBN: 979-8-9997784-0-6
Paperback ISBN: 979-8-9997784-1-3
e-Book ISBN: 979-8-9997784-2-0
LCCN: 2025917429

Cover and inside design by Natalie Stokes-Peters
(On Point Book Design; www.onpointbookdesign.com)

AALBC.com LLC.
15310 Amberly Dr, Ste 250
Tampa, FL 33647
troy@aalbc.com
Printed in the United States of America

DEDICATION

I AM DEEPLY GRATEFUL for the opportunity I've been given to serve, to lead, and to love. Among my greatest blessings, alongside my beloved wife Valerie, are my incredible children and grandchildren: my amazing son Jonathan; my two beautiful daughters, Jaclyn and Janna; their wonderful husbands, Jermon and Stephen, whom I consider my own; and my seven precious grandchildren—Ava, Asher, Maxwell, Joah, Sophia, Joyce (Joy), and Jourdin. They are my heart, my joy, and my living legacy.

And to Ural L. and Lucille Golden, Louis and Edrena Golden, and Napoleon and Alice Williams, this book is also a tribute to you. Your wisdom still echoes through my thoughts and choices today. You taught me that the color of my skin was not a limitation, but a responsibility—to lead with excellence, integrity, and compassion. You reminded me that selfishness would never be rewarded in the long run, and that a life of service produces joy, peace, and fulfillment that can't be measured.

Samuel P. Golden

CONTENTS

Introduction IX

Prologue XIII

Second Chance Sam 1

For the Love of Granny 9

Heaven-sent 21

Momma's Love 24

Beyond Color Lines 39

For the Love of Valerie 41

Mean Green Forever 53

No-neck Sam 60

That Fateful Night in Bealmont 67

Tough as Nails 72

Time Well Served 77

A Treasured Friendship: The Greatest Dividend of the Financial Crisis 89

A Giant Among Men 94

Family, Faith & Mentorship 99

Sunshine 103

Beyond Mentorship 107

The Power of Ditty through the Presence of Dad 110

Growing up Golden 114

Count It All Joy 117

Epilogue 121

Our Golden Family Tree 128

Photo Gallery 132

Words of Wisdom 143

Acknowledgements 167

INTRODUCTION

ON MARCH 17, 2022, I celebrated my seventieth birthday—a milestone that filled me with quiet joy and deep gratitude. That morning, like so many before it, began with prayer. But this time, my prayers carried a deeper sense of reflection. Reaching "threescore and ten" wasn't just a marker of age; it was a living testament to God's grace, mercy, and faithfulness throughout my life.

As I prayed, my mind drifted back to the journey, from my early days as a boy growing up in Wharton, Texas, to the many chapters that followed. I thought about the people, the lessons, and the moments—humbling and triumphant—that helped shape who I am. With Smokie Norful's *"Dear God"* playing softly in the background, I felt a divine nudge whispering to my spirit: *It's time to tell the story.* That song has long been a spiritual anchor for me, reminding me that no matter the circumstances, I always have a reason to be thankful. We played it at my retirement celebration from the Office of the Comptroller of the Currency (OCC) in 2008, marking the close of a thirty-four-year career in public service. Yes, I had the extraordinary privilege of helping to build and lead the OCC's Office of the Ombudsman, a role created specifically for me, in an organization grounded in fairness, integrity, and service. I worked alongside some of the most dedicated professionals I've ever known, and together, we made a meaningful difference in the lives of thousands of consumers, bankers, and colleagues.

As part of the OCC, an organization tasked with overseeing national banks and federal savings associations, with a focus on ensuring the safety and soundness of the national banking system, I learned the business from the ground up. I conducted bank examinations, which included the often intricate task of reviewing interest rate and liquidity risk calculations; ensuring compliance with the Community Reinvestment Act and fair lending laws to prevent discriminatory practices like redlining; assessing the quality and effectiveness of Board oversight and management supervision, among many other things. Under the Clinton Administration, the Office of the Ombudsman was created to resolve complaints within the national banking system and serve as a bridge between regulators and banks when disputes arose. I was honored to be appointed as the first person to lead that office.

Even now, as I write this, I'm overcome with emotion because I know without a doubt that my life has been a series of divine appointments. They've all been opportunities to use my God-given gifts in service to others. I've held many titles: National Bank Examiner, Field Manager, Ombudsman, CEO, Board Chair. But none compared to the roles I cherish most: Husband to Valerie, Dad to my children, and Granddad to their children.

On my seventieth birthday, my daughter Jaclyn gave me a letter that was so authentic, heartfelt and inspiring that I found myself reading it over and over again in the days that followed. I have included the letter at the end of this Introduction. In her words, I saw the truth I've long held in my heart—that my life has had purpose beyond positions and accomplishments. Her letter confirmed what I already sensed in my spirit—that this story needed to be told. Her words solidified my decision to write this book. Not only as a tribute to the God who has guided me throughout this journey called LIFE, but also as a legacy for the generations of Goldens who deserve to know where they come from. If not for God, and as a tribute to all He has blessed me with, then for my family and the generations of Goldens who will one day stand on the foundation we've laid.

This memoir is my offering. A testimony to the life I've lived, the values that have shaped me, and to the people, many of whom I'll name in these pages, most of whom have stood beside me, lifted me, and held me accountable. I'm so grateful to my parents, Ural L. and Lucille Golden and to my grandparents, Louis and Edrena Golden, and Napoleon and Alice Williams, who taught me that life must be lived with purpose, passion, and faith, and modeled the "3 D's": Desire, Discipline, and Determination, the principles I've done my best to live by and which I will expound upon in future chapters. They showed me that true stewardship is not about personal gain, but about using your time, talents, and influence to serve others, even those who don't share your last name.

This book is for my family, my friends, my colleagues, and those I may never meet. It's for anyone who believes that legacy isn't built in a single moment, but in a life lived with intention. And it's especially for those walking a path they may not yet understand and who need to be reminded that God *does* order our steps, even when the road ahead is unclear.

So, welcome to my story. My hope is that these pages won't just offer a glimpse into my life, but that they might even serve as a spark that causes you to build a *golden legacy* of your own for the ones you love and cherish most.

I am thankful for the presence of mind to understand that life is more joyful when lived with passion, purpose, and faith. And I recognize it is now my duty to extend that same impact to those who will follow.

Jaclyn Golden Malone

March 20, 2022

Dad,

What an amazing milestone! God has blessed you with threescore and ten, a testament to the faithfulness of His promises. In your 70 years, you have seen so much, done so much, and are a lot of things to so many people. But I have the privilege of calling you, Dad! And you have played that role also well. As busy as you were, you always put us first. You were at every game, tournament, and event that you could make. You have been supportive, encouraging, and reassuring. The. Best. Dad!

While your list of accolades and accomplishments is a mile long, the greatest things you have taught me are that life is not all about me. I see by your actions that the more the Lord elevates you, the greater the call to serve others. I have watched you model this behavior my entire life. And I am not just talking financially. You are generous with your time, wisdom, and resources. People who come into contact with you are blessed beyond measure.

Thank you for just being you...

Thank you for always prioritizing your family.
Thank you for leading by example.
Thank you for being the best Paw Paw to Joah and Joy.
Thank you for the love you show Jermon.
Thank you for raising us to trust God and raising us in church.
Thank you for showing me the beauty of a 44-year marriage.
Thank you for letting me tag along with you and your boys on Saturday mornings on the golf course...and thank you for not letting me quit in college (haha).

When I began writing this letter, I was so thankful that I didn't have to make up nice things to say. You are the same person at home as you are at work, as you are at church...as you are everywhere you go. You operate with integrity which makes giving you your flowers so easy.

Your Right,

Jaclyn Golden Malone

PROLOGUE
by Dr. Michael S. Sweeney

TIME IS ELUSIVE. And it is everywhere. It even mocks us as we try to manage our own daily lives and schedules, because it operates on a deeper psychological level than conscious effort can generally reach. An appreciation of and an acceptance of nature—especially human nature—are the best paths to its rewards, and lead to an affirmation of what most of us who are trying to pay attention ultimately grasp: more than on the strength of any individual runner, the race is won with the exchange of the baton. For those of you who will read this book in a future I will never see, you should know that this runner is not just any runner, and the friends, people, and loves in his book are not mere travelers.

Let's just get past this: I'm biased. Sam Golden is a lifetime friend, and he is the finest man I know. He wrote this book to pass the baton, and, like those who handed it to him, he succeeded in handing this baton to you in better condition than when he received it. But I know his heart, and it seems, though he never said as much, that he wants more than that from us. I sense that both he and Val want us to *feel* all that their remarkable journey conveys.

In George F. Will's book *The Conservative Sensibility*, he notes that Federick Douglass' biographer Timothy Sandefur describes "history-deprivation" as an instrument of control that made slavery uniquely brutal: "History is a shared tradition about one's origins and the glorification of the achievements of ancestors, which gives one a sense of purpose and a role in the progress of the world. History can generate pride and solidarity among a people." Moreover, "lacking a conception of their part in the progress of a nation or a people, enslaved people were encouraged to regard themselves not as dynamic and full of potential, but static and fixed in the landscape. If a slave could be deprived of a past, he could not imagine a future."

But someone (or ones) in a wretched yesterday kept a fragment from the original baton secretly close to their heart, and over time, through persistence and faith, layers were added to it until a new one was created. From a tiny unbroken core of an unremembered and faraway era, identities were established and recorded, and opinions could be openly discussed (with someone other than the Almighty) regarding such substantial issues as morality vs immorality, love vs hate, fear vs hope, and the significance of virtues made possible by freedom, liberty, and happiness. The pursuit of happiness, one of life's purposes, was joined by the ancestors of the Golden and Anderson families. Those ancestors, some of whom were by circumstance keeping their event horizons close and did not have the comfort of thinking about posterity, were giants upon whose shoulders we *all* stand—especially their offspring. Here's the point: Time stands still for no individual portrait; tomorrow the present will be history, but history—particularly this history—is powerful. For descendants, it is a living, hard-won, fundamental part of you. It should be celebrated by us all.

After forty-nine years of professional exposure to human hearts, blood vessels, and insides, I can say with certainty that whatever physical differences between us appear on the outside pale in comparison to our commonalities. We all feel pain; we all bleed red. In a silent darkness, we are virtually indistinguishable. Without a doubt, as we progress further into the light, we shall find that the same is true, as science is God's handiwork revealed. A former patient of mine was Wernher von Braun, the father of rockets and modern space flight, who told me, "But must we really light a candle to see the sun?"

Values, as mere choices, are inexpensive to acquire and available to scoundrels and saints alike. Hitler had values. George Washington had virtues. When Martin Luther nailed his *Ninety-five Theses* to a church door, he asserted the primacy of private judgment—conscience. There is a golden thread of magnificent thought connecting this important German theologian to his namesake, a Black American minister, a thread connecting his *Ninety-Five Theses* and Dr. King's "Letter from a Birmingham Jail."

Ethical lives are lived by people of good character, pursuing virtues like self-control, moderation, responsibility, friendliness, prudence, courage, and industriousness. We gather from the studies of philosophy, literature, and history that character like this is acquired slowly, often painstakingly by good habits and imitation. But even education and experience lose some significance unless devoted teachers use them to inform the future. Sam and Valerie believe that history, unlike a piece of furniture, is paradoxically more polished if left unvarnished.

If not convinced, the ancient philosopher Plato was at least optimistic that the more perfectly future generations were educated, the more perfect life would be. Being more sanguine about the potential benefits of an elite education, America's Founders instead channeled his protégé Aristotle and aimed not for perfection but for the humble attribute of happiness. They conceived of happiness the way Aristotle did, believing that pursuing a virtuous existence is the key ingredient to achieving happiness. As a dynamic, deep-rooted spirit of ongoing satisfaction with life derived from both individual reasoning and engagement with a community, happiness is not a condition but an activity. It requires doing something, and as such requires sustained efforts and patterns through living a life of determination to develop one's full potential and not merely seek pleasure.

These things do not come to us by chance. First, we need an understanding that there is an essential human nature, endowed by the Creator and common to us all, conveying moral agency and gracing us with natural rights and dignity that are both universal and inalienable. And second, that we have the liberty—not just the freedom—to pursue happiness as we choose, with equal opportunity for equal benefit. A redfish is free to go where he is inclined. Humans alone can have liberty. We are thinking creatures who can choose how we shall be inclined, and reason about the proper use of freedom.

Samuel Patrick Golden has a talent for happiness. He has virtues, not just values. He has been taught the relevant fundamentals and has felt both the glory and the occasional sadness of cultivating them. He achieved success by finding humanity in the deadlocked shadows, making the world better rather than worse as he went along, looking for a way to be kind in a world that sometimes favored the cruel and the disingenuous. When he took the baton he could feel the love, the hope, and the power of those who held it before him, and it gave him the strength to run his triumphant portion. Still and all, he knows that if the premise of identity politics is true, then the idea upon which America rests is false. If, as some new thinkers in today's America insist, social structures and impersonal forces make both individuals and history, then individuality and freedom and liberty are discounted. And these new historians are denying people's ability to rise above determinism and modify the trajectories of their lives. There is something awfully small about one who cannot see that someone else is exceptionally large. I believe that Sam's ancestors join us in celebrating this history and the Golden journey as an elegant victory, and I hope that his descendants and others will study it for magnificent inspiration.

With love and admiration,
Dr. Michael S. Sweeney

SECOND CHANCE SAM

LIFE FOR ME HAS been full of second chances, starting from when I was a young boy growing up in Wharton, Texas, relishing in the simple joys of just *being* and becoming. Today, I start each day by including in my morning prayer: "Lord, thank YOU for granting me chance after chance after chance and then again another chance!"

At one point, before I even knew the true meaning of words like *Faith, Mercy,* and *Grace*, I thought I was invincible. Take the time that me and my buddies—Ike Holmes, Skipper Ross, and Kermit Brown—had our first near-death experience. When we were eight, nine, maybe ten years old, the outdoors was every-thing to us. The moment school let out, we'd race home, legs pumping and backpacks bouncing, just long enough to kick off our shoes, change clothes, and head right back out. Most days, we met up in my grandfather's backyard or played in the quiet streets near our houses, all of which sat just a few hundred yards from the Colorado River.

One afternoon, someone got the idea to dig a tunnel. Not just a hole, but a real tunnel into the steep bank along the river. It sounded like the perfect kind of adventure, just risky enough to feel exciting. We figured we'd keep going day after day, digging until we reached Elm Street on the other side. So that's what we did.

Each afternoon, we arrived like clockwork, hauling shovels, sticks, broken broom handles—whatever we could get our hands on. We dug side by side, the river flowing just a few feet below, dirt piling up behind us. The tunnel stretched nearly twenty feet by the time things came to a stop. Pa Po, my grandfather, Louis Golden, had started to get suspicious. One day, he quietly followed us and caught sight of the tunnel. He didn't waste time. He gave us a stern talking-to, the kind that left no room for argument, then sent us home with a clear warning: "don't go back." That night, it rained. By morning, the tunnel had collapsed completely. We didn't say much about it, but we all knew what could've happened if we'd been inside when it gave way.

Looking back, I still shake my head. We thought we were just having fun—but that was one of those moments where something bigger seemed to be looking out for us.

So, when I think about the goodness of God and the life He has blessed me to live, along with *all* the second chances He's given me, I am not just emotionally overwhelmed, but extremely grateful. Another one of those second chances came in 1997 when, as a ripe and vibrant 45-year-old, I was diagnosed with prostate cancer.

The doctors discovered it during my annual physical exam when a PSA test, which is a blood test used to screen men for prostate cancer, was included as an integral part of my blood work. I credit not just the PSA test, but having it done in conjunction with the digital rectal exam I underwent, for saving my life. Since that diagnosis, I have become almost an "unspoken spokesman" for the importance of such testing, which a lot of men—both young and old—try to avoid at all costs, even if it ultimately costs them their lives. But I also recognize the fact that we, as men, can be so stubborn and bullheaded sometimes that we don't go to the doctor like we should and try our best to avoid any process or procedure we perceive as a threat to our manhood. And that is why part of my testimony and mission is to eliminate that mindset by sharing my experience and outlook on this usually curable disease when detected early.

So, in response to my rising PSA levels, my family physician sent me to a urologist to perform a biopsy. Initially, my biopsy showed atypical cells, but not cancer. But within six months of the first test, I took a second test and it was atypical again. It wasn't until about three months later, in August of 1997, that I received my prostate cancer diagnosis.

The news came around 10:00 a.m. from my urologist. At the time, I worked for the OCC, and was in my downtown Houston office when the call came in. As stunned as I was after I hung up, I immediately went to God in prayer, asking Him to cover Valerie and our children with His love, grace, and mercy. I also made a special request by asking for His amazing healing power. Once I gathered myself, I made the call to Valerie, who was then, and still remains to this day, MY ROCK. I could tell from the other end of the phone line that she was doing her best to choke back tears, as she managed to reassure me with her comforting words, "God will take care of you and our family, honey. We will get through this just fine."

The next call I made was to one of my dear friends of fifty-six years, Dr. Michael S. "Mike" Sweeney. Mike is an extremely accomplished cardiac surgeon, who I had the blessing of growing up with in Wharton. His initial response, when I gave him the news, was a chuckle. Needless to say, it caught me off guard, but then came his words of reassurance, "God has too much in store for you and you're too tough Sam. Besides, you're gonna die from something else, not this."

We both chuckled.

"Now hang up this darn phone and I'll call you back in a few minutes."

So, there I was, with a spouse and three young children to raise, and a grim cancer diagnosis. But God was certainly on my side, along with my friends and family, whom were determined to give me all the love, encouragement, and resources to get me through this storm.

Within less than forty-five minutes of receiving the call that no one wants to ever receive, Mike called back to tell me I had an appointment at 2:00 p.m. that day with Peter Scardino, one of the top urologists and prostate cancer surgeons in the nation. I made a quick call to my urologist's office to give authorization to have my records couriered over to Dr. Scardino's office, before placing a call to Valerie to share what had transpired since our conversation earlier that morning.

"Praise God," was all she could manage to say through her muffled cry.

Fast forward to 2:00 p.m. that afternoon, Valerie and I were seated in front of one of the best prostate cancer surgeons in nation. It was nothing but the grace of God that got me there, in front of Peter, where I was supposed to be.

As a forty-five-year-old Black man, statistical odds were stacked against me, but God's favor was all over me. Because of my age and the fact that prostate cancer is typically extremely aggressive in young Black men, my options were extremely limited: watch and wait, radiate, or extract. Peter already knew that the best option was to have surgery to extract the cancer. And in his professional opinion, it was the only logical option. He informed us that impotency and incontinence were both possibilities, two of *any* man's biggest fears, but as hard as both the diagnosis and prognosis were to hear, Valerie and I welcomed Peter's candor and agreed to proceed with the surgery.

"You have young children. If we don't do this, their dad won't be here," Peter explained. To which Valerie, without hesitation, responded, "I married this man because I love him and I want him living. I love HIM, my children love him. Dr. Scardino, you do what's right."

Her words made the tears that had already formed in the wells of my eyes fall and stream down my face.

The surgery to remove my cancer was on October 17, 1997 (exactly twenty years prior to the birth of my grandson, Joah). I was the first patient that Peter had performed this type of surgery on, involving nerve grafts. He grafted nerves from my right ankle and transferred them to the area adjacent to the prostate gland to materially lessen impotency issues. Not only did Peter and his skilled team of surgeons save my life, but they also focused on saving the quality of my life, for which Valerie and I are both grateful.

I am proud to report that it's been twenty-eight years since my surgery, and I've had no issues. Every day of my life I fall to my knees when I get up, and before I go to bed. Why? Because I'm blessed and know the purpose God has for me. That purpose is to be a vessel in the lives of others, just as Mike and Peter were to me. If this weren't true, I know God would've taken me out long ago.

A few months after the successful removal of my prostate gland, Peter called me to ask if I would consider attending a luncheon with Bill Rohr, another friend and patient of his, who was also a prostate cancer survivor.

"The two of you can collectively change the lives of other men, particularly Black men," he said. "With your combined passion and know-how, the two of you can do some amazing things to get the word out about this disease that is raging among Black men."

His words resonated with me and Bill, who was a retired senior executive with Chevron Chemical at the time, and is now at rest with our Heavenly Father. Together with the amazing support of Barbara Payne, we formed and led an organization called Prostate Action, Incorporated for eight years, with a mission to educate men, particularly in minority communities, on prostate cancer and the importance of early screening.

Since all of this was before the Internet and the World Wide Web were a thing, most of what we did was paper-based, but together we created a communication plan. With the help of an expert team, and partnered with Methodist Hospital in Houston and other community leaders, pastors, and professional athletes, we hosted a citywide Prostate Cancer Awareness and Testing Day at Houston's George Brown Convention Center in 1999, which was a huge success. In fact, I truly believe that men are alive today because of our organization.

My third "second chance," as I will refer to it, came a few years later in 2002 when my son, Jonathan, was a sophomore at Baylor and played running back for the Baylor Bears. I had planned to attend his spring football game but noticed some blood in my stool a few days before. Being a man on the go as I was and have always been, I didn't think anything of it. In hindsight, I know now that blood in your stool is never normal. If you see it, say something; or better yet, do something about it.

I remember feeling lightheaded on the drive down to Waco from Sugar Land, where we lived at the time, but assumed I was tired from working all day that Friday. Thankfully, I thought better of it and set up an appointment with my gastroenterologist as a precautionary measure. When I got back home that evening, I mentioned my lightheadedness and bloody stool to Valerie, who insisted I go to the doctor right then and there. I reassured her that I was one step ahead and had already made an appointment for Monday morning at 7:45 a.m., which seemed to quell her concern. So off to bed I went, exhausted from my trip.

The next day, God allowed me to make it through not one, but two church services, as well as the drive back home, when I felt lightheaded to the point of almost passing out. I also found more blood in my stool. That night, after resting a while but with conditions not improving, Valerie refused to take no for an answer. The commander of my house and my heart insisted that we go immediately to the emergency room, to which I agreed.

My intent was to shower before heading to the ER, but God had a different plan. I don't remember much, just that I passed out on the shower floor. By God's grace, both Jaclyn and Janna were home and although Janna, who is a heavy sleeper, slept right through it all, Jaclyn heard the commotion and, at Valerie's request, immediately went next door to get our friend Evelyn Shearer-Poor, who is a pulmonologist.

By the time the ambulance got me to the hospital, I had lost so much blood that they had to give me an emergency blood transfusion—seven units of blood, to be exact. It took the doctors three days to find out where all the bleeding was coming from, which was an area right below my esophagus. Initially, they didn't know if I had a tumor in my colon or if the bleeding was coming from somewhere else. They inserted a tube down my throat to cauterize the bleed and then gave me another blood transfusion. I was hospitalized for five days total and haven't had a problem since.

Once again, God saw fit to spare my life, which could have easily been cut short due to the amount of blood I lost. So, when I say that I know that God is real, please believe and know that I am a witness to His goodness and grace and will forever give Him praise and thanks. He's an almighty God!

Now whenever I look into the precious and innocent little faces of my grandchildren, who have no idea what my life's journey has been and everything I've been through, the depth of my emotions sometimes overcomes me, just the mere fact that I'm still here with them. And, of course, I'd never want them to know or endure the pain or struggles I've experienced, some of which I will share in these pages; yet and still, I want them to understand the blessings behind them all. Our God is AWESOME!

I truly believe that what you instill in your children and your children's children, and the generations that follow, will be a part of your legacy and what they will ultimately pour into their own children and so on and so forth. As I enter my *Golden* years and what I anticipate will be the best and most fulfilling years of my life, I plan to do just that; starting with the legacy of my grandmother, Alice Williams, and my parents, who taught me how to love God and others without condition and also poured into me some of life's greatest lessons and blessings...

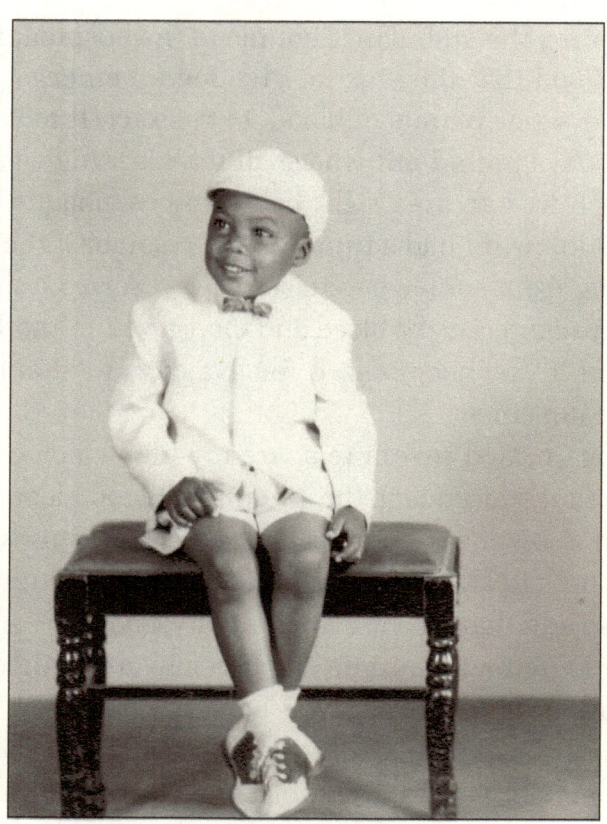

Sam in his Easter outfit (1955)

For the Love of Granny

THEY SAY THE GREATEST gift you can give to someone is your time, but I beg to differ. The greatest gift is not just your time, but more importantly, your *presence* and undivided attention. The notion of "being present" did not always come instinctively for me, but instead was a learned behavior that was skillfully taught to me, over time, by my good friend and executive coach, Jo Ann Lucero. It was also lovingly demonstrated very early on by my grandmother, who poured countless hours into me. No distractions, no expectation of return, no complaints, just her precious time. It always brings to mind the many conversations I've had with my dear Valerie and her constant reminder that, "People don't give a damn about you being the CEO of anything, Honey. All they want is your time and for you to show up and be fully present during the time you extend to them." This, along with countless other reminders lovingly drilled into my head and heart by my late, wonderful Grandmother Alice, is what keeps me grounded to this day.

Born on June 18, 1896, my maternal grandmother, Alice Williams, whose framed face is one of the first faces I see each morning when God wakes me, blessed the world with her presence for ninety-six years before she went home to be with the Lord. Although God blessed me with two very special grandmothers, my paternal grandmother, Edrena Golden, perished when I was only nine years old. As such, my memories of her are not as vivid and impactful as those with my maternal grandmother, but her footprint on my life is ever-present, nonetheless.

I called my grandmother Alice, "Granny," and she, and almost everyone I grew up with, called me "Skippy," which Mother named me from the womb because I kicked her throughout the pregnancy. I cannot recall a day growing up that I did not see my precious Granny. Our homes were, at most, less than a mile away from each other, separated by Highway 59, one of the few major highways that intersected the tiny town of Wharton, Texas. Her house at 1027 W Burleson Street was the last house on the left-hand side, and adjoined a pasture which separated it from the Colorado River. And in Granny's backyard was Grandaddy's dog pen where he kept his hunting dogs.

Just beyond the pasture was a rendering plant. Now if you are not familiar with what a rendering plant is, just think of the worst, most rank smell you've ever smelled in your entire life and multiply it by ten. There is nothing more rank because it is where they take all the unwanted remains from cattle and hogs to transform them into bioproducts. You got used to the smell, but on days the wind came out of the South, it reminded you what it meant to grow up on *the wrong side of the railroad tracks*, as they say.

Historically, and even sadly still today, low-income Black families often live in the undesirable and just plain ugly parts of the community, whether it be across from an eyesore like railroad tracks, in close proximity to dangerous and unsightly power lines, near petrochemical plants, or amidst the stench of a rendering plant. But what I lacked in aesthetics growing up as a child, my grandmother made up for in love. That woman cared for and loved me in ways that cannot be qualified or quantified. But I'll do my best to explain...

From the time I was old enough to ride my bike until the time I was able to drive, I made my way down to Granny's house for a daily dose of love, the best cooking on the planet, and the most incredible lessons that life had to offer. Granny worked as a housekeeper for the Chatham family, a well-to-do white family in Wharton. She was also a housekeeper at the Davis Hotel, where she made the beds and mopped the floors, among other duties. During the summers, the harvest season, she also picked cotton to make extra money. Incredibly, she could pick between 300 and 350 pounds of cotton daily. In fact, from the time I was able to take mental note of it, Granny worked hard and tirelessly, yet she always managed to find time to spend with me. That is the type of grandparent that both Valerie and I have set our sights on being. There was something special about my relationship with my Grandmother Alice because of what and how she poured into me, and I strive to have that same type of relationship with all seven of our precious grandchildren.

Between her and my grandfather, Napoleon Williams, who worked as a porter and wrecker driver for Cochran Buick Motor Company in Wharton, my maternal grandparents made an honest living that put food on the table. But not just any old food. I'm talking about the best food on the planet. Yes, Granny was an absolutely *amazing* cook. Cooking was her therapy, in a sense, and an escape from the toils of her daily life, which included mistreatment and disrespect by hotel patrons.

Every dish she made was prepared from scratch, including her coconut pineapple cake, which was my favorite. This woman was so serious and meticulous about her cooking that she even grated the coconut for the cake by hand. She never cooked with anything from a bag or a can.

In simple terms, my Granny was an exceptional woman in every way and the most unselfish person who gave so much to so many people. Many examples come to mind, but the way my grandmother poured into so many of the families and children in her community has and always will resonate with me the most, and I remember thinking, *why is she doing all of this*?

Again, my grandparents worked menial jobs all their lives and had little money. They lived in a very modest one-bedroom house with an outhouse outside. Eventually they were able to save enough, with help from my parents, to add a second bedroom and an indoor bathroom. The things we take for granted were luxuries to them. But despite having so little materially, Granny was always so willing to share with those who had much less than she, not only giving to her family, but also to her church, her community, and even to strangers. She had such a benevolent heart and, although I didn't realize it then, I now realize what a blessing it was to bear witness to, and ultimately emulate, her same way of living. She was so many things to so many people, but even with her busy work schedule and endless hours volunteering at the church, she still managed to spend time with me.

Granny was extremely dedicated to her church, Macedonia Missionary Baptist Church, which was about three blocks from her house. The church, with its pinkish-red brick, was positioned on risers as protection from flooding. In fact, when Hurricane Harvey came through in 2017, Macedonia was one of the few structures on the west side of Wharton that did not suffer massive destruction and flooding because of those five-foot risers. And praise God that it still stands, unfazed and unbothered and with all its holy splendor, in its original location.

As the "mother of the church," as Granny was so honorably and affectionately referred to, on any given Sunday you could find her in her usual spot, which was on the left-hand side of our humbly small church, on the second pew from the front.

As her one and only, and *favorite* grandson, you could find me stationed right there next to her.

At the ripe, young age of eight, I made up my mind I was ready to join the church. I remember that one Sunday, as Pastor Rueben Robinson gave his closing remarks in preparation to open the doors of the church to membership, I felt an urge to respond to his invitation to welcome God into my heart. I don't know what I was thinking, but no sooner had his lips parted to ask if anyone in the congregation was ready to give their lives to the Lord, that I sprang from my seat and marched right up to him, standing front and center.

As Pastor Robinson looked down at me with wise eyes and a smile that could warm the coldest of hearts, I felt the gentle grasp of my grandmother's hand behind me and her distinctively high-pitched, but pleasant, voice gently whisper, "Oh, I'm so sorry, pastor, but he's not ready yet."

One thing anyone knew for sure about my Grandmother Alice was that although she had one of the kindest, gentlest, and most loving spirits known to mankind, she was also stern and no-nonsense when it came to her faith. But she was also very nurturing, not just in a motherly type of way, but also spiritually in the way that she explained and broke down the Word and teachings of God, and especially in the way that she lived her life.

But my feelings of humiliation and dejection from being turned away at the altar were quickly transformed into knowledge and understanding. After church, Granny took her time in explaining that I was making the most significant choice I would ever make in my life—more important than the close second of choosing whose hand I would take in holy matrimony one day. To her credit, she didn't snatch me up that day to scold or embarrass me, but rather out of love and to prepare me for the most precious, intimate, and long-lasting relationship I would have in my lifetime outside of those I have with my wife and family—the one with God, and his Precious Son, Jesus. In fact, she explained that my actions were not just about joining the church, but more so about accepting Christ as my personal Lord and Savior, which was a HUGE commitment.

"It's not a game," she told me, with a stern tone but loving disposition. She wanted to make sure I understood the significance and what I was committing myself to. Over the next six weeks or more, Granny spent time with me nearly every day, teaching me the Word and ways of the Lord, and praying with me and for me, on what she referred to as her "praying ground."

Granny's praying ground was at the foot of a massive, full-grown pecan tree that sat just across the pasture, a few yards from the banks of the Colorado River. On days that I rode by either on my way to her house or to another one of my pit stops around town, I could hear her distinctive, high-pitched voice praying in the distance; a voice powerful enough to command the stillness of the air and stop the swaying of the trees.

We spent a lot of time there, confiding and praying, praying and confiding. She explained her relationship with Jesus, the struggles she had encountered, and how Christ navigated her through it all. Little did I know that the same struggles she encountered as an uneducated young Black woman growing up in the South, I would also encounter in the boardroom as an *educated* young Black man trying to climb the ladder of success in a white man's world of privilege and power.

So, due in part to the basic tenets and building blocks of faith that my parents, whom I will speak more on later, had already instilled in me, Granny was not starting from scratch. As I sat there listening to her day after day with an open mind and eager heart, I often wondered how she was able to speak with such veracity, wisdom, passion, and love. What I thought was a secret formula, was actually God's anointing on her life. After my six weeks of listening, absorbing, praying, and repeating, Granny and I both knew that the time was right. I was ripe and ready.

Once again, it was a typical Sunday morning at Macedonia. Granny and I were stationed on the second pew on the left and my mother had also joined us for church that morning. Pastor Robinson had just delivered one of his typical, soul-stirring sermons and was about to open the doors of the church to new membership and communion with the Lord. This time, instead of springing up and making my way past Granny, I laid my hand on hers and, heart pounding, studied her for even the slightest indication of permission. She returned my stare with that gentle, loving smile of hers along with an approving nod. Simultaneously and ever so subtly, she positioned her legs to allow me to pass.

Heart still pounding, I marched proudly in the direction of the pulpit where Pastor Robinson stood. He looked at me, smiled and then looked just over my head and behind me, at my grandmother. I didn't look back, not from fear of Granny, but from full confidence that I had her approval and that I was ready.

Her words from behind, "He's ready," along with muffled giggles from the congregation, as if everyone remembered what I had done six weeks prior, were all blessed reassurance that I was, in fact, *ready*.

The feeling of Pastor Robinson's hand on my shoulder stopped the pounding of my heart, and the eminence of his voice was enough to command stillness from the audience. I couldn't muster up a word, so instead I tightened my already closed eyes, and cried. At just 8 years old, I was filled with the Holy Spirit and it was one of the most blessed days of my life.

I'll never forget the pastor's words that day, "Skippy, there's nothing more special than the love of a grandmother and what this woman has poured into you, young man, you will cherish for the rest of your life."

And I did just that... For the remainder of Granny's days, until she went home to be with God, I cherished her. And I now cherish her memory and her spirit, which lives through me today. Looking back now, I can remember thinking that day how enormously blessed I was to not only have the love of my parents and grandparents, but also the love of God, who loved me so much that He blessed me with His Holy Spirit, which lives in me even as I spew my heart out onto these pages. One of my favorite gospel songs by Chester D.T. Baldwin, "I Still Hear Mama Praying," reminds me of how incredibly blessed I am to have been reared by a praying Mother and Grandmother.

From that day and beyond, my relationship with my grandmother soared to even greater heights, as we shared a new kinship of sorts in our individual and collective spiritual experiences. She escorted me into a Christ-filled life, which I am forever grateful for. As I grew in age, maturity, and stature, and through my pubescent, adolescent, and even adult years, she taught me the importance of living an unselfish life, and one of impact, in terms of touching the lives of others. She also encouraged me to give more than I received. Again, Granny had very little money and a first-grade education, but the love, knowledge, and wisdom she provided to me and others, whose lives she also poured into, were more precious than gold.

"I never saw a Brinks following a hearse," she used to say, leaving me bewildered at the time, furrowed eyebrows and all, even though I knew the vans with "BRINKS" written on the side were full of money. But as my age grew in digits, I began to understand the importance of it in that it's not about the money you leave behind, but about how you positively impact the daily lives of others, and the legacy you leave for others to carry.

She also used to tell me, "Skippy, every day, be sure to touch the life of somebody that doesn't have your same last name." And she used to say, in that sweet voice of hers, "Remember Skippy, somebody's always watching you. When you do good things, you impact the lives of others and it contributes to making the world a better place."

Such simple and impactful words from a simple, impactful woman of God. Words that resonate and ones that I've shared with even my youngest of grandchildren—not to scare, stress, or put pressure on them, but to let them know that when you live your life in a way that glorifies God, and do things constructively, in a positive light, and in proper order, you can have more impact than when you live your life destructively.

These were just a few of the principles I was raised on. Granny poured so many of these precious nuggets into me and, through this book, I will do the same with my children, grandchildren, and their children's grandchildren, as well as generations of Golden children I'll never meet...

Granny always did what she thought, in her heart of hearts, was the right thing to do and set such an unbelievable example for me and others, by making unquantifiable sacrifices, which ultimately opened up the windows of understanding and opportunity for me. Believe me when I say that there is nothing more impactful than to have another person who loves you, without condition, pour into your life. That's exactly what my grandmother did until the day that she took her last breath.

As the years passed, I started and finished college, which was a monumental experience and achievement I will speak on later, and although I married my beautiful wife and moved away from Wharton, I was never too far away, or too busy, to make time for Granny. When I worked for the Office of the Comptroller of the Currency (OCC), I traveled extensively, but still saw her every chance I got, including many weekends, and some weeknights too, when I was examining banks near Wharton. Valerie and I lived over an hour and a half from Wharton, in a northeastern suburb of Houston. Some weeks, I would leave work and drive the hour-and-a-half-long trek to check on Granny and drive back home—praise God for travel grace and an understanding wife. Some nights my head wouldn't hit the pillow until midnight or later, but my Granny, just like my wife and children, was a priority.

In 1992, we moved to Sugar Land (located immediately southwest of Houston), which was closer to Wharton and made the commute a little less unbearable. This move occurred right around the time that Granny's health started to deteriorate. To ensure that she was properly cared for while I worked and traveled, I had to retain help in the form of the sweetest older Black lady, named Ms. Viola Jenkins.

Ms. Viola was a family friend who resided on the same block of Burleson Street as Granny, and helped to cook and clean at her house. Although I continued to climb the ladder at the OCC and make good money, I didn't have to pay Ms. Viola a fortune, which was a blessing with five mouths to feed. Ms. Viola helped us out tremendously and I finally felt a sense of relief that my battle to achieve some semblance of work-life balance was over. Until, that is, Granny called me one day and said, in her usual nonchalant tone, "Hey Skippy, just wanted you to know that I fired Viola."

My mouth dropped first, followed by my head and then my shoulders, as I gripped the phone and intently listened to what came next.

"Two women in a house ain't ever gonna work," she said. "Besides, it's my house, not hers."

As sweet as my Granny was, she became feistier as she aged. She was ninety-two or ninety-three at the time, and just as stubborn and independent as I can be sometimes at my age. I neither argued nor tried to reason with her but after we hung up, I called Ms. Viola to apologize and thank her for her time and service. Once that was settled, Valerie and I immediately went to work in search of finding Granny more suitable living arrangements.

It wasn't long before God blessed us in our search with an assisted living facility that was brand spanking new. Granny loved Avalon Place, and it was right there in Wharton, where she had vowed to live and die. Needless to say, she quickly became the "Queen" of the nursing home. She was loved and adored by everyone and lived there comfortably for nearly four years, until April 1993, when she went home to be with the Lord.

The last day of her earthly life is forever etched in my memory. Granny called me that morning and in a noticeably weak voice said, "I'm tired Skippy."

"Oh, Granny," I said, asking no questions but knowing full well that the time had come. I called Valerie, as I always do in times of triumph and crisis, and immediately left my office in Houston to drive to Wharton. Granny was already at the hospital, which was next door to the nursing home, by the time I arrived.

I made it to her room and sat by her bedside in just enough time to see her pass away. But before she perished, she managed enough strength to raise her head, gently grasp my hand, and look into my eyes with her usual warm, reassuring smile, which instantly put me at ease.

"I'm at peace baby," she said. "I'm going home to see Jesus."

I tried my best to fight back the tears. And I succeeded for the time being. But the lump in my throat grew with each word that she spoke.

"That house of mine, you essentially give it to a woman with a rotten husband, or no husband at all, cause you and Valerie are never coming back to live in Wharton. And you look in the mirror every morning and look at the person you see staring back at you and what we talked about on those praying grounds, okay?"

"Yes, ma'am," was all I could manage to say before she took her last breath.

Since that fateful spring day in the little, tiny town of Wharton, Texas, I have not felt that level of pain and personal loss. I imagine it being comparable to the same type of pain that Granny herself felt years prior when she lost my mother, her only child, who was only fifty-nine years old at the time of her death.

I remember my drive to Wharton that day, from Houston, and my struggle to piecemeal words to communicate the news of my mother's passing to Granny. I was already torn up about it myself, but I knew that it would devastate Granny. Valerie and I had no children at the time and I could not fathom the thought. The impact of losing a child and her only baby I thought most certainly would take her out. But being the strong, God-fearing woman that she was, my Granny looked at me with tears streaming down her face and said, "Nobody but Jesus...thank you Jesus for her life."

Needless to say, I was stunned by her words.

"I'm gonna be fine," she added. "She's gone home to be with Jesus and I'm gonna be just fine because I know that Jesus will take care of her," to which I replied, "And I am gonna take care of you Granny."

And that's exactly what I did. I praise God for His provision and His divine blessing of precious time...

Sam's maternal grandmother, Alice Williams (1945)

Heaven-sent
by Estella Grant

TO THE TINY TOWN she was born and raised in, she was known as Mrs. Alice Williams, but to me, she was my beloved Aunt Alice and the closest I've ever come to experiencing an angel here on earth.

My Aunt Alice was married to my uncle, Napoleon Williams, which technically made her my aunt-*in-law*. But I considered her more of my "aunt-in-LOVE," because of the unconditional love she showed me, as if I were one of her own. I lost my mother when I was just twelve years old, and upon learning of her passing, Aunt Alice came to our rescue. We didn't have much and neither did she, but between her and my grieving father, they made sure that my five sisters and I were well taken care of in the days following our devastating loss. She took care of my home and of my heart, during one of the saddest, loneliest, and most confusing times of my young life. That was just the type of person she was, and the type of person she raised Skippy to be as well.

While the world knows him as Sam and Mr. Golden, we knew him as "Skippy," which I still call him to this very day. Skippy is just an amazing person, just like his mom and grandmother were, but he was quite the character growing up. There is a fifteen-year age gap between us, with me being much older than he, so the only thing Skippy and I really had in common was our love for Aunt Alice. She was crazy about Skippy and he was just as crazy about her.

Not too long after my mom passed, Dad moved our family from Wharton to Bay City, Texas. Thankfully, it was only a twenty-minute drive, which meant we could visit Aunt Alice on most weekends and sometimes she would drive down to visit and check on us too. I simply adored her. Out of us six girls, I felt that I was her favorite, likely because I was named after my grandmother, who was also her mother-in-law. Our special bond meant that I would always get to stay a little longer, whenever I asked, and often got to spend my summers at her house too. Skippy and I can laugh about it now, but at the time, he didn't like the fact that I spent so much time with his Granny, especially at her house, which was like his second home.

"Why do all those girls have to come over here? I don't want them here. When are they leaving?" he would often ask.

"Skippy, don't act like that," Aunt Alice would lovingly tell him, but in a scolding tone and with a side-eye.

During those summers that she confirmed I would be staying with them, his response was usually one of disappointment: "She's staying for the *whole* summer Granny?" he would ask her, nearly in tears. "Well, when is summer gonna be over?"

For the most part, Skippy and I managed to stay out of each other's way, but he made it very clear that he didn't like playing with us girls. Ironically enough, we are now the best of cousins and the best of friends. Skippy looks out for me in the same way that he did for Aunt Alice, for which I am grateful and blessed beyond measure. He took care of her when she couldn't take care of herself, and I would expect no less because of the example Aunt Alice set for him.

Sam and his grandmother had a special relationship like none that I've seen in my lifetime, and I can say, without a doubt, that her legacy lives on through him—in the way that he lives his life and loves on his family, and through his commitment to God and to a life of service dedicated to helping others.

Sam's beloved cousin, Estella Williams Grant (2010)

MOMMA'S LOVE

NOW THAT YOU UNDERSTAND the significant role and impact that my grandmother Alice had on my life, I would be remiss if I did not pay homage to my parents who, by God's hand, gave me LIFE. My mother, Lucille Williams Golden and my father, Ural Lincoln Golden, as well as my paternal grandparents, Louis and Edrena Brown Golden and maternal grandparents Napoleon and Alice Williams, were all a part of the village I credit with not just raising me, but molding and shaping me from the soft, impressionable lump of clay I was as a child, into the loving but firm and bold man of God that I am today.

Collectively, *my village* gave me the willingness to dream BIG, accompanied by the courage to stay the course when the storm winds blew. In an unwavering way, they insisted on my steadfast walk of the "3 D's" (**Desire, Discipline and Determination**). First starting with **Desire**: they taught me early on the importance of having goals, both short and long term. "You must know where you're going in order to get to where you want to be," Granny always said. Which is why I've always urged my children, mentees, and subordinates alike to give serious and frequent thought to their goals, particularly as they sought out opportunities, whether it be in their personal or professional lives. Said very simply, YOU MUST WANT IT!

Secondly, when it comes to Discipline, it may sound trite but it's definitely true: "In life, there are NO free handouts, son. No one is going to *give* you anything." These words my father instilled in me as a young man still whisper to my spirit from time to time even as a seasoned adult. That's why when opportunities are presented, I'm always prepared to take advantage of them. Prayer, preparation, discipline, and diligence have always been critical components of success. Opportunities may abound, but if you're not prepared, you may very well lose out on a potential step in your progression. Discipline is necessary to maintain the often rigorous course that will confront you. There are many demands and distractions that you'll be faced with along the way, but that's where prioritization comes in—it goes hand in hand with self-discipline.

Lastly, I would be remiss if I failed to emphasize the importance of Determination. Sometimes, despite my best efforts, my parents and grandparents always told me that I would undoubtedly encounter frustrations and obstacles in my quest to fulfill my goals. This is LIFE.

"However, do not allow your determination to be diminished or swayed because of these encounters. Your ability to succeed is limited principally by your own effort. A change in the road does not necessarily mean the end of the road...after all, if you don't believe in you, who will?" they always said. Their wisdom was incomparable. My advice? If you discover that you're discouraged by a delayed event in your life, seek a mentor or others who have embodied the success that you desire, which is often what I've done throughout my life and career in order to bolster my determination. You will find that you must remain committed to your goals, believing in yourself regardless of the circumstances.

Lastly, they taught me *never* to feel entitled to what I had not earned. And they never let me forget that selfishness was not a part of their journey (or mine) and that I should prepare myself, at all costs, for the race that would give me a greater capacity to give more.

My parents had me later in life when my Dad was thirty-six and my mom was thirty-one, during a time when most folks were having kids in their teenage years. I was their only child and often wondered, *Why just one, why just me?* But out of respect for their decision, I never asked them why they didn't give me any brothers or sisters. Inherently I knew that, in spite of being an only child, I was exponentially blessed with a village of cousins, and even neighborhood children, who became my brothers and sisters.

I could not have asked for a better mother than Lucille Golden. Unquestionably, it was my mother's care, love, and discipline that shaped me into the person I am today. She was a doting Mom in every sense of the word, and as her only child, she poured into me immeasurably. Now this was quite a feat considering the countless children I shared her with over the thirty-three years she taught in Wharton's segregated and unsegregated school systems. Momma was a great teacher who was unbelievably disciplined. She was sweet as pie, but tough as nails too, when she had to be. She taught third grade for most of her tenure and cared about her students both inside and because teaching was not just a way to pay the bills for her; it was her calling.

Momma was truly her mother's child. Like Granny, she was a God-fearing woman who, along with my grandmother, made sure that along with my grandmother, I was in church every Sunday, despite the fact that we sat on opposite ends of the church. Yes, Momma typically sat on the left side of the church, on a middle aisle, whereas, as I've shared before, my grandmother and I sat on the second pew adjacent to the center aisle of the church. Momma was the epitome of servant leadership. She truly walked the walk. Among the countless, priceless things about my mother I can recall are how patient, encouraging and understanding she was. She knew what a unique and special relationship I had with her mother, my grandmother, and whereas most mothers would be embarrassingly envious, Momma was just the opposite. She encouraged my and Granny's inseparable relationship and was grateful to her mother for partnering with her and my father, along with my godmother, Aunt Emma Gordon, a High School English teacher, in my education and rearing.

I credit my mother for my inherent ability to not only talk to people of all colors, creeds, and backgrounds, but also to be able to relate to them because as she and Granny always used to say, "We're all God's children." Despite the odds they faced in a hyper-racist society back then, neither of them ever allowed hate or defeat to take up real estate in their hearts. I also credit my natural ability to speak without hesitation or fear, in front of thousands of people, to Momma. In fact, she always insisted, whether it be in school or in church, whether at a school play or church musical, that I step up and flex my "talent muscles" in order to step out of my comfort zone and into the spotlight. She was always there to help me when needed, but also made sure I was challenged when it came to working independently. All of these ingredients have served me well in creating, in me, the leader I've become.

We weren't rich people, so my parents didn't have much materially to offer me, but I honestly cannot imagine growing up in any other home that was more loving than ours. My parents loved me through their words and through their actions. And although my father loved me and I loved my father, I would've also loved for him to be around a lot more than he was. You see, my dad and his brother, my Uncle Eddie Louis Golden, owned liquor stores in Houston—Uncle Ed's in Houston's infamous Fifth Ward on Lorraine Street, and Daddy's in Trinity Garden. Due to the sixty-mile drive that separated his store and our home, we only saw my father on Wednesdays and late Saturday nights. On Sundays we'd all get up and go to church; however, Dad attended a different church than my mother, grandmother, and I, and had been doing so since they were married in 1949. On occasion, I would also attend Mother Zion Baptist Church with my father, paternal grandfather and great uncle, Sam Golden (who I'm named after), but admittedly, I wasn't too keen about the fact that we all didn't attend church together especially since we always seemed to have such limited time together. As a child, and still now, I wanted to savor every single ounce of time, love, and attention that was afforded to me.

Not having my father around a lot gave me the desire and drive to spend more quality time with my own children when they came along. In fact, I remember early on, even before Valerie and I were married, making a pledge to myself that if God ever blessed me with a loving wife and children, I would be present. And despite the fact that most of the roles I've had throughout my career have required an immense amount of travel, I have always made it a point to make sure I got home as fast and as soon as I could, and to make sure that when I *was* at home, I was present. At times, that sacrifice called for me to commute at ungodly hours, to make sure I was home when my children awakened in the morning so that mine and their mother's faces were the first ones they saw and so that Daddy could take them to school most mornings.

Lots of children grow up and never know their fathers the way I knew mine, so I realize how fortunate I was to have both parents, despite the fact that Dad wasn't around as much as I would have preferred. Whatever time I lacked with him, Momma certainly made up for it. She became one of my dearest friends in life as I grew into adulthood, yet she always made the distinction between mother and child known. No one can love a human being like a mother can. I know who I am, but the relationship I have with my children, although very special, is no comparison to Valerie's relationship with them. In the same manner, I realize and accept that I'm not their mom.

And while I didn't have that same close bond with my father as I did with Granny and Momma, I am ever grateful for the presence he played in my life and the hand he and my grandfathers had in molding me into a man. He unequivocally made it known that he wore the pants in our family. In fact, he used to say, "Son, there are two male figures in this house and ain't but one of them is a man, and that's not you."

Through his and my mother's influence and their innate ability to run a household through structure and guidance, I have been able to provide that same structure to my household and I am a firm believer that if you let your children run your home, you will most certainly have an unhappy one. Why? Because, at the end of the day, parents must be parents. I had parents and grandparents who weren't my best friends when I was a child growing up, but I always knew I could count on them for provision and protection. And protectors they were, especially Momma. She never wanted me to play the game of football, which later became my passion sport and meal ticket into college, because it was too dangerous in her eyes. "Just keep playing baseball, Skippy," she would lovingly admonish, "football is too rough."

But like every child back then and even now, I was determined to go my own way and ended up trying out football for size—and it fit. I made the team in seventh grade. And because the junior high and high schools were on the same campus, Coach Wanza would occasionally let us practice with the high school teams. I used to do pretty well in comparison to my player peers, so much so that Coach Wanza thought and even vocalized to others at times, *"This kid is gonna be pretty darn good."* I ended up securing a longstanding role as a running back because I was always reasonably fast and rarely got injured, which is why my mother finally gave in and allowed me to continue playing. With that, I went on to high school as a pretty decent football player.

Around 1966 is when the integration of schools in Wharton and many other places around the state started to occur, right as I entered high school. Momma was one of the first teachers they asked to teach at the newly integrated schools, and of course, it seemed only natural that I go with her.

As a teenager, I was pretty headstrong and set in my ways. I loved my life and was comfortable with my standing and status within my own Black community of friends and family, so naturally I wanted to stay put where I was, where I was comfortable. I refused to be a guinea pig for integration, but needless to say, my father shut down the notion of me staying behind pretty quick.

"Last time I checked," he said, looking me in the eye, "there was only one man in the house, son, and it's not you. You're going to that school."

All things considered, going to the integrated Wharton High ended up being a good decision because up until that time, I hadn't really spent any time around white folks and didn't have a single white friend. My mother was my biggest cheerleader and fan, so she knew that I could do anything I set my mind to do and had no doubt I would compete just fine with the white kids, and that I would fit in just fine too. She didn't want me to be concerned about being made a mockery of, and she made it clear that nobody was gonna run over or take advantage of either of us.

Although Wharton High had advanced classes for freshmen, I wasn't placed in any of them. Instead, I was placed within the traditional classroom setting along with the handful of other

Black kids who attended. Since Momma had been an elementary school teacher for most of her tenure in education, she didn't know a lot of the teachers at the high school, but she knew the district superintendent, and he knew her well. She didn't understand how was it that several of my deserving Black counterparts and I weren't placed into AP classes, so she took her case to the Wharton High School principal, and within a matter of days, several of my friends and I were in AP classes. It took courage on her part because she could've kept her mouth shut and let us get through high school operating under the status quo that everyone was accustomed to, being Black. But she wanted us to be challenged by a learning environment that would ensure we were well-prepared, and in some cases, even better prepared than some of the white students.

Now when it came to my white counterparts, once the culture shock wore off and reality set in, I became more comfortable associating with and even befriending them. The sweet spot came when the walls of racism were torn down and long-lasting friendships were born—like the beautiful friendship that evolved over time between my lifelong friend, Robert Taylor, and me.

Robert was the first white person I ever befriended. His mom was also a teacher who had become friends with my mother early on in their education careers. I'll never forget that first day of my freshman year at Wharton High. Just as the release bell rang, Robert, a complete stranger, walked right up to me and said without hesitation, "My mom said we need to be friends."

My response, and the only appropriate response at the time was, "Okay." And just like that, we became friends and are still dear friends to this very day.

Again, Momma always had my best interests at heart. She sacrificially gave of herself to ensure that I had the best of the best, including ample opportunity to excel. When the counselor at the high school suggested I prepare myself to be a long-haul or Mack truck driver, my mom was furious! She quickly *corrected* the counselor and even suggested that she take a look at my academic record before she suggest such a thing. Not that a truck driver is not an honorable profession, but Momma knew it was not the career path that I'd be on. However, between her and my father, they made sure that I was multi-faceted. Momma and I used to spend our summer months, when school was out, at our family house in Houston. And once I got into my junior and senior years of high school, Uncle Leon would pick me up and drop me off to work with a nice white gentleman named Mr. Edgar Q. Smith, who he worked for as a handyman on occasion.

Mr. Smith was the retired General Counsel for Humble Oil, the predecessor company of ExxonMobil. He was also the owner and CEO of EQ Smith Enterprises, which was a privately held company with ownership of multiple small office buildings in the Houston area, a Christmas tree farm, a large ranch in Grimes County, TX, and multiple apartment buildings. It was through my work with my Uncle Leon and Mr. Smith that I learned how to do master electrician work, master plumbing, tiling, roofing, etc. These invaluable skill sets have assisted me greatly in my life's journey and made me the multi-talented man that my mother aspired for me to be.

Fridays were always paydays for us and Mr. Smith insisted that he pay me directly, as opposed to paying me through Uncle Leon. This practice taught me how to value and manage my money. On many occasions, when my uncle dropped me off and went to pick up sandwiches for us, Mr. Smith and I would have man-to-man mentoring visits where he would confide in me, "I love your Uncle Leon, Sam, but I have a feeling that you're gonna be a businessman and not a handyman. Your future doesn't include manual labor, but trust me, in the business world, you'll work a lot harder."

In hindsight, I think Mr. Smith was among the first men, other than my Dad, my uncle and Grandfathers, to serve as a mentor in my life. In fact, every Friday, he set aside time to sow wisdom into me during our "talks," while my uncle made a food run to the Burger King located at Kirby Drive and the Southwest Freeway in Houston. I know now that the time was orchestrated by him and Uncle Leon, as it was just long enough for Mr. Smith to shower me with the nuggets of wisdom, tidbits of encouragement, and sprinkles of knowledge. I always left with a lot more knowledge than I had coming in. I am so grateful that through my connection to, and the actionable love of Mr. Smith, I am now blessed to share a lifelong friendship with his son, Ashley, and his wife Peggy.

Long story short, I ended up making "All-State" in football my senior year, which led to earning a scholarship to attend the school of my choice. Yes, my football skills helped to pave the way for an education that my parents could not fully afford. Praises be to God. Mom and Dad were determined that I would get a college education, but the fact that I earned a full athletic scholarship was a game changer for my family. Again, we didn't have much to begin with, so it would've made life burdensome for them if they had to scrape up money for me to go to college.

I made visits to a long list of colleges that were on my personal wish list including ones that sought after me such as Stanford, Rice University, Texas A&M, and the University of Texas at Austin. When Mr. Smith learned that the aforementioned colleges hadn't honored my request to have someone from the College of Business counsel me on their programming, he said I should insist, and that's exactly what I did... But despite my numerous requests to other colleges and universities to meet with a representative from their respective Colleges of Business, the University of North Texas, known as North Texas State University at the time, was the only school to oblige, making my decision that much easier.

Sam signs his Letter of Intent to play football at North Texas State University, witnessed by his beloved high school coach, Eddie Joseph. (May 1970)

Sam's beloved mother,
Lucille Williams Golden (1955)

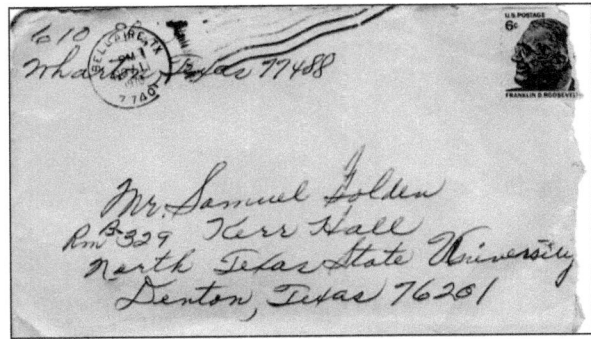

First letter from Sam's mom when he started college (Fall 1970)

Sunday Eve;
Dear Skip,
It was nice to hear your voice. I always feel a lot better when I know you are O.K. Thought once you wouldn't call.

Glad to know you are enjoying the car.

Daddy said you didn't have much money so I thought I had better send my little bit.

The Tigers won another game only by a hair. The score was 7-6 Bowen made the TD and Garrett Martin was most valuable

player according to
Coach Porter on Tiger
Talk Saturday morning.
I'm sure you will
read about it in your
paper next week.

Mrs. Moore says Beverly is
interested in attending
North Texas another school
year. Don't think
Marge heard a word
she said.

Jewel and Leon come
out today, also Aunt Lucille.
They found the eggs
Everyone is O.K at home.
Very little happening, so
I can't gossip with you
much this time. Maybe
I'll have more to

Till you the next time.
Say hello to Charlie, and
you all try to stay
away from the dope,
and all persons
connected with it.

Love,

Momma

P.S. Be a good boy

Before Sam went to North Texas State in 1970, his mother gave these to him:
"Worthwhile Values" on the back of bank deposit slips

-The greatest handicap - Fear
-The Base Day - Today
-Easiest thing to do - Find Fault
-The greatest Stumbling Block - Egotism
-The greatest Comfort - Work Well Done
-The most Disagreeable Person - Complainer
-Best Teacher - One who makes you want to learn
-Greatest Need - Common sense
-Meanest Feeling - Regret of another's success
-Best Gift - Forgiveness
-The greatest moment - Death
-Greatest knowledge - God
-The greatest thing in the world - Love

5 - BEYOND COLOR LINES
by Robert Taylor

I MET SAM, also known as "Skippy," in 1966. We had an immediate kinship and quickly became the best of friends, teammates, and classmates, graduating together from Wharton High School in 1970.

Our mothers were friends and shared long careers as teachers, a role they both loved and were passionate about for most of their lives. Despite our obvious difference in race, Sam and I were destined to become friends because of how we were both raised. Probably the most enduring and important quality we shared back then, and even now, is our respect for *all*—regardless of ethnicity, education, religion, or background. I grew up outside of Wharton, Texas in the extremely tiny town of Pierce. There, my childhood friends and I were as close as we were diverse in that we shared a colorblind mentality that enriched each other's lives, despite the fact that we came from varying ethnicities.

People often ask Sam and me about the challenges we faced as friends at a newly desegregated high school back in the '60s.

Between the two of us, we can think of a few obstacles except, of course, when it came to our lives as both athletes and scholars. Unquestionably, Sam was confronted with situations where he was treated differently because of the color of his skin, but he consistently rose above them with a smile. While he and I were challenged on and off the football field, by the same token, we also challenged each other to be the best in *every* endeavor we took on, whether individually or collectively. No doubt, Sam made me a better person, a better athlete, and a better student. The handful of positive attributes I may have passed on to him undoubtedly pale in comparison to the thousands he has bestowed upon me.

Post-graduation, Sam went on to UNT, but we have remained friends through the years and see each other when we can. I am grateful that our families, wives, and lives are intertwined forever and feel confident in saying that I *truly* know Sam Golden because I know his heart. He is a man of God and mirrors God's example in word, thought, and deed. Through the years, Sam's friendship has enriched my life and is one of the blessings for which I am most grateful. I have no doubt the world would be a much better place if there were legions of "Sam Goldens" in our midst...

For the Love of Valerie

AMONG THE COUNTLESS BLESSINGS I am grateful for, surely the one that reigns supreme is the gift that God bestowed upon me, the day I met my beautiful bride of forty-eight years and counting. Valerie is unequivocally *my person*, as the young people say. While some may marvel at history's greatest love stories, whether they be Cleopatra and Mark Antony, Johnny Cash and June Carter, or, one of my personal favorites, Barack and Michelle Obama—I have no doubt that Valerie's and my journey will go down in our family's history as one of *the* greatest love stories of all time.

Few are blessed in this life to have found the love of a woman who will truly stand by you through thick and thin, and everything in between, but I have found that and so much more in my sweet Valerie. In fact, for the entirety of our romance, I have treated her with the same love and respect as when we first met. I buy flowers even when there is no special reason, just to show her that I love and am thinking about her. I try to show Valerie in some way that I love her each and every day. I also pray for her daily, and it has been my constant and consistent prayer that through all the seasons of our lives, God will bless our union and continue to strengthen our bond. I am fully aware that I am not in my first, second or even third quarter of my life. I am in the fourth and final one, but whether I live another twenty years or not, I pray that God takes me first. Why? Simply put, because I can't imagine living a life without her.

Valerie and I are nearly three full years apart in age. When I was a senior, she was a freshman. While we didn't have many encounters in high school, I remembered her as a skinny, petite little thing that stood about 5'2" with a beautiful face, infectious laugh, and lovely smile. It was the 3rd of June, that day I will always remember. It was the day I first met Miss Valerie Anderson. She was a breath of fresh air. The weather was not especially hot that day in Wharton, Texas, but below our usual ninety-degree temperatures. She looked like the woman of my dreams, and I instantly knew I had to go for it. Valerie lived about three miles east of Wharton, in what is known as the Dinsmore community, which is a very small, close-knit, and 100% African American. Valerie is the fifth of six siblings, and while we had several friends in common, I was closest to her older brother Alfredie, and her sister Estell, as the four of us were closer in age. Additionally, we all shared a mutual friend in Arthur Edwards.

Arthur Edwards was one of my closest friends, known by all as Arthur Lee. He lived directly across the street from Valerie's family with his grandmother, Ms. Mandy Edwards. Since, of course, we didn't have cell phones back then, I always took my chances when stopping by on a whim and, almost always, he was away. There was one day in particular back in 1972 that I fondly recall as the day that young Valerie first caught my eye. Everyone seemed to be out and about, watering their yards or sitting on their porches. I drove to Dinsmore and stopped by to visit Arthur

Lee. Once again as usual, he was not at home; however, Valerie's mom, my dear, late mother-in-love, Mrs. Velma Anderson, was stationed on her front porch in the distance, within eyeshot of where I had parked my green 1970 Dodge Challenger.

"Hi, Mrs. Anderson," I hollered from across the street. I waved and she smiled. "Is Alfredie home?"

"No, he's not here," she replied. "None of the boys are here."

"What about Estell?" I asked, as I walked across the street and approached her, hoping my trip hadn't been entirely wasted.

"No, no one is here but me and Valerie. She's on the side of the house reading her magazines."

I recall that I had not seen Valerie in some time, so I thought the proper thing to do was to at least speak to her before I set off to make my rounds around Wharton and surrounding small towns. I made my way around to the side of the Anderson house to the carport where Valerie sat. Just as Mrs. Anderson had said, her head was buried between the pages of her reading materials, but that's not what caught my attention. Instead, it was the pair of red-and-white-checkered hot pants that Valerie donned that day along with her beautiful, radiant, and somehow more mature smile than I remembered, that made me feel something I had never felt before in our encounters, which had been few and far between. The little ninety-two-pound (when soaking wet) girl from years past had blossomed into a beautiful and cutely curvaceous young lady. I thought to myself, *Man, she is fine, she has really grown up*. To say I was amazed by her transformation is an understatement.

Long story short, an exchange of awkward *hellos* led to a three-hour conversation that day on the side of the house under the Anderson's car port. By the end, I found myself completely smitten and reluctant to walk away without the promise of another opportunity to see her again. With fear in my heart, but an imaginary "S" on my chest, I mustered up the courage to ask her to go to the movies with me. Although her response was disappointing, it was expected because of our age difference and her upbringing.

"You're wayyyy too old for me, Sam Golden," she responded in that soft voice of hers. "No, I don't think so."

In the blink of an eye, I knew it would be time to head back to North Texas for football camp, but even with this brief encounter, she was already consuming my thoughts. The next week, I went to see Arthur Lee with the hope, intent, and anticipation of seeing Valerie again. It was almost the exact same scenario—Arthur Lee was not at home, for which I was grateful, and Mrs. Anderson was on the porch, but this time Valerie was in the house asleep. The butterflies in my stomach rose up the moment she came to the door. She was still as beautiful as the last time I saw her, if not even more so. I didn't go inside, instead asking her to join me outside. We casually strolled around to the side of the house near the carport, where this time I immediately asked her to go to the movies with me. Once again, she declined.

"Nothing's changed. You're still too old, Sam Golden," she said.

Two weeks later, I returned with more determination in my heart and the offer of a ride in that old green Challenger of mine. My hope was to spend a little more "talk time" with her, with the goal of negotiating a formal date. Countless hours of long talks, and weeks went by before Valerie finally accepted my offer of a date and to court her properly.

Here is how that went.

"Valerie, I know you keep saying that I'm too old, but I have two tickets to see Michael Jackson and The Jackson 5 concert in Houston in a couple of weeks and I'd love for you to join me," I offered. Her eyes lit up. Watching her reaction, I instantly began to smile with renewed optimism.

I hoped that she would have a change of heart, with my offer to see the hottest group on the planet at the time. I prayed it was an offer too good to pass up.

"Well," she paused, "I'll have to talk with my mother first. I will have to let you know." I waited patiently...about two days, before calling her, and the answer was—YES.

I also knew that her dad might have something to say about it. Everyone who knew him was terrified of him. When I saw Mr. Anderson, I gave him a firm handshake, straightened my shoulders, and looked him straight in the eye. "You take her and bring her back immediately after," he said, in the most intimidating voice you could ever imagine.

"Yes sir, I promise you," I responded, without breathing or blinking. "That's exactly what I will do."

Valerie and I had the most incredible time of our lives on what we'll always recall as our official first date on July 23, 1972. It was about 11:00 at night when we were able to get away from the venue, the Sam Houston Coliseum. We drove to my parents' home in north Houston and spent the night, in separate rooms of course. We got up, had breakfast with my parents, and then headed back to Wharton.

However, before taking her home, I had to stop at my granny's and grandpa's home so that I could introduce "my girl" to them. I was already so serious about her. As much as I did not want our date to ever end, I remembered Mr. Anderson's words and an imaginary shotgun in his hand as I walked her to the porch. Needless to say, I wanted desperately to kiss her, but I refrained. However, I was pleasantly surprised when she leaned in to kiss me on my cheek before she smiled and told me how much she really enjoyed the Michael Jackson and Jackson 5 concert and our time together.

And the rest, as they say, is history and the making of a beautiful relationship.

I returned to North Texas a couple of weeks later with the impression of Valerie's kiss implanted on my cheek and the memory of our magical night together in my heart. However, before leaving, I gave her my high school senior class ring as my promise and commitment. She accepted it proudly and wore it on a chain around her neck. I promised I would come and see her every chance I could, and send her letters and call in between.

I did all of that happily. Stamps were eight cents back then, so it cost little to send her letters and cards every week. I shared my days with her on paper, mostly recounting my week of classes and long football practices. I was a pretty popular guy on campus and had lots of friends, but managed to keep my nose clean by staying out of trouble, studying hard, and playing football even harder. I had too much to lose not to. And since I was raised to have a heart to do things that were right and pleasing to God, my grandmother's teachings were always at the top of my mental toolbox. I was not perfect, and admittedly did things that I'm not proud of today during my time at North Texas State. However, I am proud to say that I made wise decisions and walked away from trouble more times than not.

Every chance I got, I would pack up my things, jump in that little green car and head back home to spend time with my family and see my beautiful Valerie. I knew she had other gentlemen suitors while I was away at school; after all, how could she not? With me away most of the time, and as attractive and charming as she was, I would've been foolish to think anything otherwise. Yet what gave me hope was the fact that she made the effort to see me by riding with her brother Alfredie to several of my football games, including Homecoming, which was very special to me.

That first Christmas in 1972, I bought her a pearl and diamond ring. A little diamond and a little pearl were all I could afford at the time. I took our relationship to the next level by asking her to *officially* be my girlfriend. Game on! My calls, letters, and visits increased exponentially, and I even surprised her by making an impromptu trip to attend her high school graduation, which was very special to both of us.

I graduated from North Texas State with four top-notch job offers, but ultimately accepted an entry-level Assistant National Bank Examiner role with the Office of the Comptroller of the Currency (OCC), which allowed me to move back to Houston and closer to my family and the love of my life. By that time, Valerie had graduated from high school and was enrolled at Wharton County Junior College. She worked hard to put herself through junior college and ultimately the University of Houston.

When she transferred to the University of Houston, she lived in a rough part of town with three other roommates who had attended Wharton County Junior College with her. The location was what Houstonians often referred to as a "war zone." But that didn't stop me from seeing her every chance I got. Between my work with the OCC, Valerie's University of Houston class schedule, and her part-time job at Prudential Insurance after her morning classes, we made it work. I can recall the words of Mr. Anderson, during my and Valerie's courtship, as he reminded me from time to time that his daughter would graduate from college. And her father had also said that when she graduated, she would do so as Valerie Anderson. He wanted his three girls to be independent and self-supporting. Yes, even back in the 1970s, fathers wanted their daughters to be strong-minded and independent.

God's timing is always perfect and so was mine. It was Christmas Day of 1976, and her entire family was home for the Christmas holidays in Dinsmore, Texas. There were a lot of activities going on with a great deal of excitement by the entire Anderson family to be celebrating another Christmas together. Her three older brothers and two sisters were all gathered around and exchanging Christmas gifts.

I was nervous as heck when I approached Mr. and Mrs. Anderson and asked to speak with them privately. I needed their permission to marry Valerie and ask for her hand in marriage. I needed...and wanted their support. They graciously gave approval with a firm handshake and a pat on the back, at which point I asked Valerie to step outside. It was chilly and drizzly outside, so I invited her to sit in my car and said something to this effect: "Valerie, sweetheart," I recall saying nervously as I grabbed her and gazed into her eyes, "we have been together for over four years. I have grown to love and respect you more than I can express in words. I wish I could kneel in the car, but I can't. But I want you to know that I can't imagine a life without you and because of that, I want to live the rest of my life with you, and I would really love it if you would marry me and be my wife."

Tears immediately welled up in the corners of her eyes and her lips quivered as she responded, "Oh yes, of course I will. Yes!"

I had saved my money for at least six months prior until I had earned enough to purchase an oval 0.9 carat ring from Houston Jewelry, the jeweler my mom frequented. At the time, the ring was only $995.00, a good deal in 1976, for the diamond itself along with the design and mounting. I placed the ring on her finger, and we sealed the deal with a kiss and long embrace before heading back into the house to make our announcement.

In May 1977, approximately five years after we started dating, Valerie graduated from the University of Houston as Valerie Anderson with a degree in Finance from the C.T. Bauer College of Business, and landed a great job with Shell Oil Company. Not long after her graduation, we were married in a small and simple wedding in Wharton, Texas. Small... Well, about 200 invited guests in a country town where you know everyone, and everyone knows you.

On July 26, 1977, the Tuesday before our wedding, my grandfather, Louis Golden, who had been ill for a while, died. My dad was insistent that we not get married and come back for the funeral, but we figured things out and held the funeral on Friday, July 29, ahead of the wedding. Later that day, our rehearsal dinner was hosted by my godmother Ms. Emma Gordon, my mom's best friend, who loved me beyond measure, and it was a great feast.

On July 30, 1977, we had a church wedding ceremony at the Mother Zion Baptist Church, officiated by a dear friend and classmate of mine, Reverend George Edwards. Arthur Lee was the best man and the one who stood by my side. This was so fitting

since he was integral in our actual meeting and subsequent dating. The fact that he was rarely home had made all the difference. As Valerie's father started to walk her down the aisle, our eyes locked, as if there was no one else but us in the entire church. When Valerie reached about halfway down the aisle, she winked at me, bringing the biggest smile to my face. *Now* we were ready to make our ultimate commitments.

We took pictures and were then off to the reception, about a ten-minute drive away, at the Knights of Columbus "KC" Hall. As we sat in the back seat on the ride over, I looked at Valerie and thought to myself, *We are finally one. I will always cherish and protect her with my life.*

It was a beautiful reception given by my parents with an elaborate buffet, drinks, and a live band—Paul and CJ Kearney and the Superiors. Our first dance was to the music and lyrics of "You Are So Beautiful." I'll always remember that Saturday night after the ceremony; we got in our Chevy Malibu and drove three hours to San Antonio, Texas to spend our honeymoon. We stayed at the La Quinta Inn, all we could afford at the time, toured the city and its famous Riverwalk, and then drove home to Houston a couple of days later since we both had jobs to get back to.

For our future wedding anniversaries, we vowed to always do something special and nostalgic. I fondly recall Valerie saying, "I want to go back to San Antonio, honey," to which I responded, "I can tell you one damn thing, sweetheart, we're not staying at the La Quinta Inn." On our fifth wedding anniversary, after the birth of our first child Jonathan, we headed back to San Antonio. This time, we spared no expense and went all out, staying at the Marriott on the Riverwalk overlooking the river.

Every year, I try to take Valerie on a new honeymoon adventure. It is not always at the exact time of year as our wedding date, but it is somewhere exciting and interesting, to celebrate our time together as a married couple. When kids came along, we tried to create memories for them as well. And boy do family vacations get expensive when your kids get married and have spouses and children. We love it though and would not change a thing.

Throughout our married life, Valerie's only requirement for a car was that it would never stop. Two different cars failed this requirement, and each time, she came home and told me the car had to go. The second time a car stopped, it was literally one block from our house in Woodforest in north Houston. Valerie got our son Jonathan out of the car seat, walked to the house, and said to me, "This car has to go. It will not get a chance to strand me again." I took care of that right away. She has never cared about the make, model, or year of her transportation. The only requirement, as I said earlier, was that it would not stop on her. I have always stayed on top of maintaining and updating our cars to ensure this does not happen.

Valerie worked hard at various jobs since her early teens, to include a hospital service person, a desk clerk and key punch operator for Prudential Insurance. The woman I married understands the value and use of money. We both believe that one should live within one's means. We never thought being house poor, car poor, or other material/stuff poor would be a successful and comfortable lifestyle as a strategy for our family. We avoided that. She looked good in whatever she wore and never needed or desired the latest high-end or designer brands. Those are the things I spoil her with.

I traveled a lot throughout my career with the OCC, and Valerie worked tirelessly to make sure our children were well cared for. She will also tell you that I came home to sleep in my own bed every night if I could, even if it meant getting home in the wee hours of the morning. It was important for both of us, as well as stabilizing for our children.

We were both extremely diligent and hardworking on our jobs. I never wanted Valerie to be overstressed between the burden of her job at Shell Oil and taking care of me, the kids, and the house. When she said she needed help, she got it. After the birth of our second child Jaclyn, Norma Cochran, a wonderful Native American woman, helped us with "Mother's Day Out" and other activities around the house. We loved Norma. She was so very kind and helpful to our entire family.

My dear late friend, Pastor Hayward Wiggins, preached it best when he emphasized that money and infidelity are Satan's primary vices when seeking to destroy a marriage. God has blessed us by protecting us from these vices.

I said all that to say, it has been a truly extraordinary journey with Valerie. I fondly recall one of the last and most impactful words of wisdom that my dad imparted upon me, on my wedding day, "Son, I will never meddle in your marriage. She's not my wife, she's your wife, but one thing I'll tell you is that you will never put your hands on her. And what it took to get her, you will have to do the same things to keep her. Even if God blesses you with children, the primary, pre-eminent relationship should always be yours and hers, not as Mom and Dad." Since then, I have come to realize that nothing in this life that is worthwhile is ever going to be easy. I recognized at a very young age that if there is something that is important to you, you must be willing to fight for it, which is exactly what I have done to preserve my marriage and family.

God has blessed us to understand and appreciate the modest wealth we have, and to use it to help others and glorify his kingdom. We believe it is a privilege, and take pleasure in supporting causes (e.g., children, education, and healthcare) that will make a difference in the lives of others. We have three children and seven grandchildren and we hope to set an example that they will strive to emulate when they are adults. More than anything, and hope to leave a legacy of LOVE for our family, that is just as rich and meaningful as the unconditional love that Valerie and I have for one another.

She is my QUEEN now, forever, and always...

Mean Green Forever

REFLECTING BACK ON MY days at UNT, they were some of the most memorable of my life and critical to the formative years that molded me into the man I am today. Ultimately, God blessed me with the connection to Dr. Nabil Aboufadel in March of 1970, when I made my first official recruitment visit. He was the finance professor they assigned upon my request to meet with a representative from the College of Business, and later became my academic advisor and mentor throughout my entire college career at UNT. Also, during my initial recruiting visit, I was introduced to Coach Rod Rusk, who was the North Texas head coach at the time and Bill Brashier, who was the Defensive Backs Coach and Recruiting Coordinator. But it was my three-hour visit with Dr. Aboufadel that sealed the deal for me in deciding my school of choice.

It was a well-known fact that most of the time, college athlete recruiting tours consisted of superficial introductions and campus tours with "buddy athletes" who made sure they showed you the best time, the biggest parties, and the prettiest girls on campus. But that wasn't for me or why I was there. Coach Brashier knew I was serious about my schoolwork from the moment we sat in his office that day and I looked him square in the eye, as I shared my dad's departing words to me.

"Son, the NFL doesn't want or need a 5'10" and 225-lb offensive guard and you'll never play pro football, so go up there and get you an education from a good school that's willing to invest in you," Daddy said.

Thanks to the extraordinary education I received in the public schools at Wharton ISD, and as one of six Black out of twelve honor students graduating at the top of our class at Wharton High, I was well-prepared for any college. I chose Finance as my major in my freshman year and Dr. Aboufadel insisted that I take multiple Accounting classes saying, "You'll thank me later Sam." In retrospect, considering some of the complicated financial dealings I've had to undertake within my long and rewarding career, I'm grateful for every difficult class Dr. Aboufadel suggested, some of which weren't even prerequisites for my degree.

Since I wasn't permitted to take my car to school until my second semester, I didn't venture far from campus much and mostly relied on my adopted village of mothers in the Kerr Hall cafeteria who fed me well, even when the cafeteria was closed on Sunday evenings. The only thing they asked in return was that I attend church. And they were more than happy to pick me up on the Sundays I couldn't find my own way. They were truly a source of love and nurturing.

For the most part, I kept my head down and was extremely focused for my entire freshman year and at least part of my sophomore year. I benefited from the kind, "yet firm mentoring of Robert Carter. Robert was a Senior when I arrived at North Texas in 1970, yet he was intentional and very direct about providing me with impactful guidance. During the third game of my sophomore year, the guy that played offensive guard in front of me got hurt, which allowed me to start every game for the rest of my college career as left guard. So, as you can imagine, I started "feeling myself," as the young people say, became a bit out of control and picked up a few bad habits along the way, which included drinking Schlitz malt liquor beer, entertaining the girls, and doing very little studying. Long story short, I brought home four C's and one B that semester. This, from a guy who made straight A's my freshman year. My GPA plummeted from a 4.0 at the end of my freshman year to a 2.2 for the first semester of my sophomore year.

I recall that Christmas holiday at home with my folks as one of the most miserable of my life. My mother hit the roof. She was so upset and disappointed that I thought she was going to kill me, whereas my dad was morbidly calm and silent. He never said one cross word about my grades during the entire Christmas break. I returned to school after the holiday season and it was business as usual with class, practice, and not much else in between. On my first day back, Coach Rusk called me prior to practice and asked me to stop by his office because my father was there. My heart sank. Something was terribly wrong. I'm thinking, *Oh God, what is he up here for; he didn't even tell me he was coming.*

Sure enough, as I made my way across the parking lot to Coach's office, I noticed my dad's little beige '59 Chevrolet Biscayne parked out front. My heart pounded as I walked what felt like death row. As I entered the building, my feet were like lead, as if 100-pound cinder blocks were attached to each one as I approached Coach's cracked door. I gave a two-knuckle knock and peered through the cracked-open door.

"Come in Sam," Coach Rusk beckoned from his desk. I saw my father sitting on the couch. As I entered, and we made eye contact. "Have a seat Sam. We've got a little bit of a problem here."

"What's that sir?" I stuttered as I took a seat next to Dad.

"Mr. Golden here says that it seems as if you've lost your focus and that your priorities are displaced."

"How so?" I looked at Coach and then directly at my Dad, who directed his gaze at Coach Rusk. The words that came next resembled an ambush.

"He says that you are supposed to be here as a student athlete but now you're more of an athlete student, but seem to have forgotten about the student component because your grades have severely declined. You brought home four C's and one B; prior to that, you had all A's, Sam."

"Yes sir."

"So, your Dad tells me that you need to refocus your efforts."

The words that followed flowed from Coach's mouth like an unyielding assault.

"Therefore, as of today, you no longer play football for North Texas State University, and he's the decision-maker."

As the tears welled up in the corners of my eyes, I managed to lift my head high enough to look over at my father, who could barely look back at me. I couldn't tell if he was more hurt, angry, or just plain old disappointed in me.

"Dad, please," I pleaded, as tears streamed down my face.

"No, son," he replied sternly. "The NFL doesn't need or want you. You're here to get a degree and nobody will hire you with a 2.2. You've got to get your focus back."

And that was the end of the conversation. I later learned that before I got there, Dad had talked to coach Rusk and explained to him just how well he knew me, his only son, and had no doubt that removing me from the football team would get my attention enough to get my grades back on track prior to the start of Spring Training. And I did accomplish that, but it was a long, hard road to that promised land, to include being completely and utterly humiliated when I was moved from my coveted second-floor space in Kerr Hall all the way up to the ninth floor, making me the laughingstock of campus. It was truly one of the most humbling experiences of my entire life, but also the greatest gift my dad could've ever given me. Why? Because he got my attention.

Midway through the semester, I managed to raise my C's up to A's and reclaim my rightful starting position on the football team, all while in the midst of pledging the premier African American fraternity on the globe—none other than THE Kappa Alpha Psi Fraternity, Incorporated. You see, I had already committed myself to pledge Kappa at the start of my sophomore year, so by the time my Dad paid me that little visit in January of 1972, I was in full-blown pledge mode, unbeknownst to my parents, who were not aware I was on a Pledge Line.

That semester was, by far, the most pressure I think I'd ever felt in my life, because not only had I already given my commitment to the Kappas to pledge, but I was equally committed to my team and, more importantly, my parents, to focus on my grades. I knew I couldn't let anybody down, but most importantly, I couldn't let myself down.

As much as I wanted to play football, I also undoubtedly wanted to be a Kappa man. And despite all the rumors of hazing that went on within fraternities at the time, I was determined not to let that happen to us. There were nineteen of us on my initiating charter line. I was #4 and given the pledge name "No Neck."

One of the nights we met with our big brothers, they tried to lay hands on us, something we had vowed never to let happen. Although most of my line brothers were large in physical stature, being mostly athletes, we were still intimidated by the presence of our big brothers. Number one, because of the reverence we had for them as slightly older gentlemen we looked up to, and number two, because of the power they held over us as members of a fraternity we so desperately wanted to join. But regardless of those factors, somebody had to take a stand, and on that partic-ular night that somebody was me—Sam "No Neck" Golden. So, with my chest poked out, shoulders back, and head held high, I stepped out of line and asked to speak. The sweat on my brow was as evident as the tremble in my voice as I tried my best not to make eye contact, saying in my sternest voice something to the effect of, "We told you up front Big Brother that you're not gonna put your hands on us."

I have no doubt the rest of my line brothers were thinking, *Oh my God, Sam has lost his damn mind.* But before I knew it, my line brother "Big Jerry," who was #19 on our line and about 6'5" and 285 pounds, stepped out of line and backed me up. From that night forward, we never had another incident again.

Marion Wilson, who everyone on campus knew as "Sugar D," was one of the brothers responsible for sponsoring the Charter or first Kappa Line, known as Zeta Upsilon, at NTSU. And he made sure that my other line brothers and I were well prepared and things never got out of hand. He was also the guiding force behind my decision to pledge in the first place and one of the coolest brothers I knew, and one I still admire and trust without exception. And not just because he drove a shiny red Corvette or was an up-and-coming business professional and sharp dresser, but because of the way he carried himself and spoke to us and about the fraternity. He made sure we knew that we were there to get our degrees and not to party excessively, and that we knew the importance of education and how serving the community was paramount to the mission of the fraternity. I knew there was a lot I could learn from him, which is why I attached myself to him, and he took me under his wing and mentored me. We remain dear friends to this very day.

My pledging journey along with my collective of experiences at NTSU under the guidance of such great, kind, and caring peo-ple as Dr. Aboufadel, the cafeteria staff at Kerr Hall, my football coaches, and Sugar D made me a believer in that it's not the singular events, but the pattern and consistency in which you pour into the lives of others, that create the impact. Mentorship truly matters and Lord knows I've had the blessing and the privilege of not just mentoring, but also, being mentored by the best of the best. I've learned over the years that when you show yourself genuinely friendly and caring to others without an expectation of getting something in return, it's amazing who God will connect you with throughout the multiple seasons of life.

Speaking of mentoring, I cannot close this chapter without mentioning my dearest friend from my college days, Clarence "Bernie" Little. Bernie and I played the same position on the football team, but our paths intersected for only one year. He was a freshman during my senior year. Most importantly, he and I were roommates, an ill-understood action by my peers. Many of my teammates said, "Sam, you're a senior and captain of our team; why would you ever room with a freshman?"

The answer was very simple; I promised Bernie's parents that I would watch over their only child. I'll never be able to thank God enough for ushering us into what has now been a fifty-two-year (and counting) precious bond of FRIENDSHIP and Brotherhood. It's so important to give the best that you have when people need you to show up the most.

NORTH TEXAS vs. LONG BEACH

SEPT. 29, 1973 • FOUTS FIELD • $1.00

Fall 1973 photo of Sam on the cover of the September 29, 1973 *Mean Green* Football Game program

No-neck Sam

by Clarence "Bernie" Little

MY BIRTH NAME IS Clarence Bernard Little, but my friends and family call me "Bernie." Sam and I first met just over fifty-two years ago, around noon on a Saturday, at a reception the North Texas Football Coaching staff had arranged at what is now referred to as the University of North Texas, in Denton. Back then, we referred to it as simply North Texas or North Texas State. Sam was among a number of players on the team who were present at the reception and assisted in the recruiting process that weekend by hosting all of us potential new players. I had been assigned another player as my host; however, during the course of my conversation with the offensive line coach at the time, Coach Andy Everest, he beckoned Sam's attention from across the room and introduced us. Our conversation was brief that day, but impactful nonetheless. In the short time we talked, I learned that Sam was from Wharton and going into his senior year in the fall as a Banking and Finance major. Sam had been recruited to North Texas as an offensive lineman and had been a starter for a couple of years already. Ironically enough, I too played offensive guard and was sure I could also earn a starting position.

As we continued to talk, looking each other "eyeball to eyeball," I noticed another thing that Sam and I had in common—we were about the same height and weight. This was ironic and unusual, given that most players who play on the offensive line are three to four inches, at minimum, taller. In fact, it was confirmation that my brief encounter with Sam that day was not by chance. Although he was called away and we had to cut our conversation short, I came out of it encouraged and inspired by Sam's energy, authenticity, and genuine kindness. Throughout my high school senior season, I had always been told that my opportunities to play college football at a highly competitive level would be very limited. So, in a sense, meeting Sam was serendipitous, but of course, for me it was just another instance of God's masterful, strategic placement of people in my life for either a reason, a season, or a lifetime. In mine and Sam's case, it is absolutely for a lifetime...

I signed my National Letter of Intent with North Texas in the early spring of 1973. My folks had only been to Denton once prior to my signing, so we all went up for the North Texas spring game in April of that year. I introduced my dad to Sam in the locker room. Their encounter was brief and very casual as they made small talk about Sam's major, his family, and his experience at North Texas. Sam was patient and respectful, and in just a matter of minutes, made a lasting impression on my parents; in fact, he was the topic of our discussion heading back to Seguin that day.

I graduated from high school in May 1973 with my intent set on heading to North Texas early, which also meant getting out of the house early, for which I was anxious and excited. Around the same time, my mother, grandmother, and uncle had convinced one of my cousins, who had just finished his freshman year at Huston-Tillotson College, to take some hours at North Texas too. It became somewhat of a family affair as he and I roomed together in North Texas' infamous Kerr Hall that summer. We were soon joined by another female cousin, who also decided to attend NT. Needless to say, Sam was one of the first people I introduced them both to.

Around the end of June, as the first summer session was about to end, it dawned on me that I would have a different roommate once the second summer session ended and fall football practice began. It seemed logical to me that I should see if Sam had a roommate, and if not, that I should ask him if he wanted to room together. To me, it made the most sense, since we were both Black football players (they generally didn't integrate roommates back then), who happened to play the same position. So why not? And when I asked, Sam charitably agreed to room with me. My parents were even more excited than I, considering the stellar impression Sam had made.

So naturally, when my parents drove up to help move me and my cousins, my mother and father managed to find some "alone time" with Sam. As I assume most parents would, they asked Sam to look out for me and to keep me on track if it looked like I was headed in the wrong direction. Of course, I was unaware of the dialogue at the time, and would have likely been offended and embarrassed had I known. Who would've thought that years later, I would do the exact same thing with my own daughter's friend, whom I met and respected enough to ask her to look after my daughter?

In late August of 1973, Sam, and I "officially," started our fifty-year friendship, that is not just limited to us, but also includes a slew of other family and friends who share in our kinship. Sam served as a co-captain of our team for the '73 season. North Texas had won only one other game the previous year and had not experienced much success prior to 1973. For Sam, being named a captain was an honor and a very important internal leadership role, especially that season. Leading and working by example, consistent adherence to standards, and encouragement of others, were all critical to our team's success that season. And Sam was a natural when it came to reinforcing those winning tenets. He always has been.

So as the relationship between Sam and me grew closer and we got to know each other as team members and "roomies," naturally we both let our guards down and even had some fun in the process, on and off the field. I think most people knew Sam by his birth name because few knew his homegrown nick-names—Skippy, or Skipper, or Skip—but the name that we affectionately gave him was "No Neck," which we'll just say is his North Texas nickname. I'm not sure who exactly gave it to him or when it became effective, but with Sam being the short, burly athlete that he was, he had an unusually thick neck. Oftentimes, we all marveled at the fact that his neck was seemingly so thick that his head just seemed to blend in and appeared to sit there on his shoulders, unassisted. Sam, being the good sport and jovial spirit that he always has been, gleefully accepted the name. He even had personalized license plates that read NO-NECK.

That brings to mind something else I admired about Sam. He had a "souped-up" green Dodge Challenger with a white top that was his pride and joy. And back then, a lot of the Black players didn't have cars, so this was quite a rarity and a luxury. In fact, during the first couple of years of knowing Sam, I always marveled at how he managed never to be the object of envy by the other guys we hung around and played with. Instead, he always seemed to generate the opposite—and that was respect. It obviously speaks volumes for some intrinsic traits that others (including myself) saw in him first, which obviously overrode any negative thoughts of envy or jealousy some, without similar benefits and background, might have been prone to have.

As one might imagine, untold numbers of things happened in Kerr Hall, our dormitory, in the year Sam and I were roommates. And while I *selectively* do not remember all the escapades of Kerr Hall living, one stands out like no other, and that was the infamous "streaking" incident. Yes, somewhere around early Spring 1974, a streaker ran through the Kerr lobby and across the campus. As it turns out, it was one of Sam's fraternity brothers who alerted us that the "streaking" would occur in the area of "The Ramps," also known as College Inn.

When Sam and I arrived, there had to be 2,000 people hanging around and lined up and down both sides of the street. For at least the next forty-five minutes or more, we witnessed a "parade" of streakers, some of whom will remain nameless for reputational purposes. Needless to say, it was among the most outrageous, yet typical college experiences I think I ever had. Sam and I laughed for days and even still to this day, especially about the chaos that ensued when two campus police officers arrived and tried to break up a crowd of over 2,000 students. Hilarious!

Back to football—North Texas, after being purely pitiful for three consecutive years, tied for the conference championship in 1973. There is no doubt that Sam's leadership that year positively influenced many on the team to perform near or at their peak, including yours truly. I know Sam impacted me.

They don't offer scholarships to players who didn't play or have individual success in high school, which was the case for me. And, as you can imagine, it was challenging to just sit and watch the first half of the season, and not even be allowed to "dress out" for home games, let alone be on the travel squad. It was easy to lose focus, not only in football but also academically and in college life, in general, but Sam's quiet encouragement helped me keep my head in the game, both athletically and academically. I could have easily gone left, stopped going to class, stopped studying, stopped putting forth effort in football, and more, but Sam's very presence helped to prevent any of that from happening. He gave me something to strive for and a model to emulate, for which I am grateful.

As the Word says, "To whom much is given, much is required." This concept is what helped to fuel my desire to do the same for others, in much the same manner that Sam had done for me. So, for the next two years, I roomed with freshmen in an effort to provide the same boost of encouragement and motivation that Sam gave to me.

Well, as the story goes, I ended up being Sam's backup during the last five games of his last season at North Texas. I'd like to think I toughened him up, knowing that if he got hurt or didn't perform, I'd be the one to take his job! All things considered, Sam and I often laugh about the multitude of similarities we share. Ecstatically, the Goldens were married in July of 1977, and me and my wife Vanessa were married that same year, in October. Sadly, we both unexpectedly lost our beloved mothers before we turned forty.

In addition, we are both prostate cancer survivors. Sam has been a survivor for much longer, since I am only thirty-two months post-treatment. But thanks to him, I was able to get a much-needed second opinion from a renowned specialist, and the best course of treatment as a result.

There is so much I want to say about Sam, but because this is his book and not mine, I digress. Sam is my brother. He is God-sent. He, Valerie and their children are family. In fact, Sam is responsible for helping me realize the dream of even having a family. You see, our daughter was adopted and, as you can imagine, adoption is a process. If it hadn't been for Sam and Valerie, who gave us a glowing recommendation and prayed for us through the process, we would never have realized the dream of parenthood and having our own family. For that, and so much more, we are forever grateful.

In June of 2023, my wife, Vanessa, suffered a stroke. We later discovered the stroke was caused by a bleed from a tumor. The tumor was inoperable and was one of the absolute most deadly malignancies. Outside of immediate family, the first person I contacted and told was Sam. Within twenty-four hours of my reaching out to him, he was here with me, praying with us and supporting me. He even saw Vanessa stand for the first time after the stroke—an occasion I almost missed, having stepped out for an hour to get a shower and a break. Sam even drove me around Austin to visit some rehab facilities where Vanessa would convalesce from the stroke.

The disease Vanessa had, usually runs a course of anywhere from months to about a year and a half from diagnosis. Throughout our journey, Sam was a constant presence with calls and prayer, wanting desperately to come visit, yet not wanting to intrude. The end came on February 10, 2024, at 2:20 am. I called Sam at about 7:00, and he was here in Austin by 9:30, just to be with me. To say that it was the most difficult day of my life would be an understatement of unimaginable proportions, but MY FRIEND was intent on helping me through it! I'll never forget the comfort I got from him that day, and subsequent days. Whether providential or serendipitous, Sam was placed in my life to show God's love and care for me. God saves only his most special angels for that.

THAT FATEFUL NIGHT
IN BEAUMONT

ON THE AFTERNOON OF May 14, 1974, I nearly floated across the stage, elated after what I considered some of the most grueling, yet rewarding years of my life. Thanks to the guidance and mentorship of Dr. Aboufadel, I exited stage left and stepped directly into my new role at the Office of the Comptroller of the Currency (OCC) on May 28, 1974. As an Assistant National Bank Examiner, I started at the bottom of the totem pole, but even then, I didn't fully grasp the magnitude of the opportunity I'd been given. Landing a job at such a prestigious entity as the OCC was truly a blessing. My assignment Duty Station in Houston, TX, included the "Golden Triangle" of Beaumont, Port Arthur, and Orange, Texas. Reflecting on it now, I know my journey with the OCC would never have been possible without the mentoring and leadership of Dr. Aboufadel.

At the end of my senior year, I had four significant job offers from major banks: First City National Bank of Houston, Texas Commerce Bank of Houston, First National Bank of Dallas, and Republic National Bank of Dallas. These positions came with starting salaries ranging from $15,000 to $17,000—a remarkable figure in those days.

"That's great, Sam, but you're not going to work for any of those banks," Dr. Abafoudel said confidently during one of our counseling sessions. "The banks will teach you how to do one thing and one thing only—how to be a loan officer."

"What do you mean?" I asked, furrowing my eyebrows in confusion.

"You're going to work for a regulator so that you can learn everything there is to learn about the industry as a whole," he replied, pausing for dramatic effect before continuing, "but not just any regulator. You're going to work for the premier bank regulator: the Office of the Comptroller of the Currency."

Through his influence and vast network, Dr. Aboufadel connected with the head of personnel for the OCC's Southwestern District and scheduled an interview for the very next day. Following his instructions, I hopped into my green Challenger and drove downtown to Dallas. I walked in sharp, confident, and prepared, answering every question with poise and even asking a few of my own.

"Well, Sam," my interviewer said at the end, "Dr. Aboufadel says you're a good guy, and since we need to hire *one of your kind*, we're going to offer you the job."

I was stunned, momentarily speechless. *Did he really just say what I thought he said?* My shock quickly gave way to anger. I kept my composure, thanked him for his time, and drove back to the University of North Texas, where I stormed into Dr. Aboufadel's office to vent my frustrations.

"I understand why you're upset, Sam," he said patiently. "But trust me—if you go to work there, work hard, and keep your head down and that man will be working for you one day."

"It doesn't feel right," I protested. "They're hiring me to fill a quota because I'm Black. Plus, the OCC's offer is only $9,931 a year. Those bank jobs would pay $15,000 to $17,000. I could make the same amount loading trucks."

"You're not meant to load trucks for the rest of your life, Sam," he shot back. "That's not who you are. You have to trust me on this. "Go there, do your job and everything else will take care of itself. In all likelihood, you'll be there five to six years max before you leave and go to work for one of those banks you're raving about, with a holistic experience and more knowledge under your belt."

His words were resolute, and I reluctantly agreed, but couldn't wait to call my Dad for a second opinion. Much to my surprise, he wholeheartedly agreed with Dr. Aboufadel's advice and reinforced the game plan for me to take the job at the OCC before pursuing one of the top banks that previously offered me roles. Never did I imagine that a five-year plan would evolve into a fulfilling thirty-four-year career at the OCC.

Undoubtedly, God ordered my steps and orchestrated my destiny. Along the way, He protected me, ensuring His plan for my life—and the hopes of my parents and grandparents—were not in vain. One of the most vivid reminders of His grace came during an incident early in my career that could have derailed my entire future.

One of my first assignments with the OCC was in Beaumont, TX, part of my coverage territory. During my time at UNT, I had a number of friends, many of whom I played football with and who lived in the "Golden Triangle" area, which was chock full of banks. It was a typical hot and humid summer evening in July of 1974, when a bunch of us decided to get together at the apartment of one of the guys who had been a former teammate at North Texas. Like typical (former) jocks, we drank beer, swapped stories, and blasted our music far too loud. Unfortunately, the noise caught the attention of a neighbor, who called the police. To make matters worse, someone had brought marijuana, and a few of the guys were smoking it. I avoided it entirely—partly because of the asthma I'd suffered as a child, and partly because I had no desire to engage. Still, I was there, and guilty by association.

When we heard the police were on their way, the smokers scrambled to flush the evidence. A loud knock at the door followed.

"This is the Beaumont Police Department. Open up!"

The tension in the room was palpable. The lingering smoke mixed with the panicked sprays of cheap air freshener and the scent of beer.

"We received a complaint about loud music," a burly white officer barked as he surveyed the room. "I smell dope. Where is it?"

Before my friend could respond, the officer cut him off. "I could take all of you n*****s to jail. Every last one of you."

I froze. It wasn't the racial slur that sent chills down my spine but the realization that I was one misstep away from prison— and the end of everything I'd worked for.

The second officer, smaller and calmer, interjected. "We're not going to do that this time," he said. "We're going to give you a second chance."

His words were a lifeline. I discreetly nudged the guy next to me, silently urging him not to speak. Thankfully, he got the message. *These guys are gonna let us go*, I thought, *please don't say anything stupid*...and he didn't.

By God's grace, we were let off with a warning. That night taught me an invaluable lesson: the fragility of opportunity and the importance of sound decision-making. I shudder to think how different my life would have been if I hadn't walked out of that apartment unscathed. And while I am extremely grateful for the blessing of God's protection that night, amongst many others, I'm even more grateful for the lesson it taught me. I was literally just a couple of months into my career, which was full of opportunity and endless possibilities. I think about how things could have gone so differently and about the heartache, disappointment, and shame it would've brought to my parents and grandparents, had God not protected me. When I think back on all the sacrifices my parents and grandparents made for me and how the situation I put myself in that night could have derailed my entire life and the plans God had for me, it makes me want to fall to my knees and shout GLORY! I remain forever grateful that he sent His angels to encamp around all of us that night, knowing full well that none of the positive things that have happened in my life could have happened if it had not been for His everlasting grace and mercy.

From that moment forward, I resolved to remove myself from situations that could jeopardize my future. I prayed for God's guidance and strength to make wise choices, knowing full well how a single mistake could alter the course of my life. That night in Beaumont was a turning point. It reminded me that God's plan for our lives often unfolds in ways we cannot foresee, and His grace is always there to guide us. Since embracing the gift of fatherhood and the blessing of becoming a grandfather, I pray daily for God to surround each of my grandchildren with a protective circle and to equip them with everything they need to make wise decisions in all aspects of their lives. I hope and pray that my experiences will resonate with them, so that when they face similar challenges, they will remember my words—even after I am gone—and always choose the right path.

TOUGH AS NAILS

ON MAY 28, 1974, just two weeks after graduation, I began my first day with the Office of the Comptroller of the Currency (OCC). The journey started with serving as an Assistant National Bank Examiner. To advance, we had to pass a rigorous, CPA-style exam covering laws, regulations, associated risks, and governance policies. Additionally, we conducted a mock board meeting, presenting a case study to a panel of five to six board members. Successfully completing these steps earned us the coveted title of National Bank Examiner (NBE).

I passed the test in June of 1978 and received my commission as an NBE. During the next few years, I went from being a National Bank Examiner, Level 1, which is what you start off as after receiving your initial commission, to a Level 2. Four years afterwards, based on my performance, I was promoted to an NBE Level 3, the highest field level at the time.

Although I was based in Houston, my initial work as an NBE 1 took me across Southeast Texas, examining small community banks. During this period, I shadowed seasoned examiners at both the NBE 1 & 2 levels, soaking up their knowledge and observing their expertise. This intentional learning phase set the foundation for my career growth, allowing me to secure assignments that would later catapult my career. I gradually began taking on more significant assignments, which included responsibility for risk assessment of the entire lending function. And, once I received my promotion to the NBE 3 level years later, I served as the Examiner-in-Charge, examining multi-billion-dollar large Regional Banks. This shift exposed me to more complex credit work, where I ensured that banks adhered to regulations and properly managed their loan portfolios—the lifeline of any bank. These responsibilities deepened my understanding of credit relationships and the risks associated with mismanagement.

While working as a lower-level NBE in East Texas, a region with a notoriously racist climate during that time, the challenges I faced were immense. On several occasions, U.S. Marshals escorted me to ensure my safety while accessing banks I was assigned to examine. To navigate these experiences, I developed a "tough as nails" attitude. I knew I had a job to do and, in retrospect, I realize how fortunate I was to have supportive supervisors and mentors who provided guidance and encouragement throughout my journey.

Mentorship played a critical role in my career. I was privileged, but more so blessed, to have strong mentors, most of whom were white men, given the lack of Black men in the OCC at that time. One mentor who profoundly impacted my life was W. Robert "Bob" Williams. Bob, who eventually became the head of the OCC's Houston office, took me under his wing professionally, and we built a friendship that lasted a lifetime. When Bob left the OCC to work at Lake Air National Bank in Waco, Texas, he became an exceptional community banker, yet continued to support me throughout my career. He was especially proud when I became the first OCC Ombudsman.

Bob's mentorship and sponsorship instilled in me a tireless work ethic. I'll never forget New Year's Eve, 1976, when we were tasked with completing a bank examination for the Bank of Galveston. I had plans to celebrate the evening with Valerie, who was my wife-to-be at the time. As the day wore on, I anxiously reminded Bob of my evening plans and the long drive from Galveston to Houston that awaited.

"I know it's New Year's Eve, Sam," he said, peering over the rim of his glasses, "but we're going to finish this exam tonight."

I hesitated before replying, "But sir...I've got somewhere to be."

He smiled knowingly and said, "Trust me, Sam. If she loves you, she'll wait."

Bob was right. I arrived at Valerie's house at 11:15 p.m., just in time to bring in the New Year with a kiss. Years later, we joked about that night, and I teased him about working me until 9:00 p.m. on New Year's Eve.

Another pivotal moment in my career came when Bob entrusted me with leading the examination of Texas Commerce Bank's multi-billion-dollar loan portfolio. Although Bob oversaw the project, he gave me full responsibility, assuring me that he'd catch me if I stumbled. His confidence in me was unshakable, and while he pushed me to excel, he never let anyone undermine my efforts. Bob wasn't just a mentor—he was an advocate, sponsor, and friend. He gave me opportunities far beyond what most in my position would receive, knowing I was willing to tackle the toughest challenges and the "ugliest" of examinations that no one else wanted to touch with a ten-foot pole. Over time, I realized there was a method to the madness. By volunteering for the most difficult, complex assignments, I built a reputation as someone who not only accepted challenges but delivered results.

"Give it to me. I'll do it," I would say.

This mindset opened doors I never imagined. Each challenge made me stronger, more skilled, and ultimately prepared me for the opportunities that followed. Before I knew it, my reputation as a subject-matter expert in the industry preceded me.

As the years went by and the banking industry evolved, challenges became increasingly significant. I vividly recall the early 1980s, when we were often called upon to assemble special SWAT teams of examiners to handle some of the most complex and demanding cases. One such case involved a small bank in Oklahoma City called Penn Square Bank. Unfortunately, the bank failed over the Fourth of July weekend in 1982. I was part of the examination team tasked with examining and ultimately closing Penn Square. That closure became a catalyst for a broader downturn, triggering a domino effect that impacted other banks and the oil and gas industry.

During this period, there was a troubling rise in "bad loans." In fact, I ended up serving as an expert witness for the U.S. Attorney in the Northern District of Illinois in Chicago, helping to bring the case to closure. From 1984 to 1988, I spent nearly four years, on and off, traveling back and forth to Chicago to prepare for and testify in one of the largest banking trials in history. Giving expert testimony was just one aspect of the job, but it was a significant one. Becoming an expert required time, experience, and a deep understanding of the industry's complexities—particularly the nuances of loans.

To explain the issues to the jury in layman's terms, I created a large board listing the thirteen loans in question on one side, with the "5 Cs of Credit" across the top: Character, Capacity, Capital, Collateral, and Conditions. Using bright orange dots, I highlighted the flaws in each loan, visually demonstrating patterns of poor judgment and outright criminal negligence. This approach helped clarify how high-profile bankers knowingly approved loans for borrowers who couldn't repay them.

Despite numerous objections from the defense, the prosecution made its case. The trial, which sent shockwaves throughout the financial services industry, concluded in 1988 with the conviction of the banking executives responsible for these fraudulent practices. It was a challenging yet rewarding experience to play a part in holding them accountable.

Time Well Served

MOVING FROM MY HUMBLE start as an Assistant National Bank Examiner in 1974, to becoming a National Bank Examiner in 1978, was far from easy. Each step forward came with new challenges. But through perseverance, teamwork, and a relentless commitment to excellence, I earned consecutive promotions, all culminating in my appointment as OCC Field Manager in 1983.

In that role, I led a large team of examiners and was responsible for examinations of increasingly complex, troubled financial institutions and holding companies across the country. It was demanding work, but critical because, after all, the health of our national economy depends in large part on a stable banking system, with bank examiners serving as key guardians. The early 1980s brought a crisis and, eventually, a crash in the financial world that was felt by companies and consumers alike. In the spring of 1982, oil prices collapsed, hitting banks in the Southwest, particularly those in Texas, Oklahoma, and Louisiana hard, many of which were heavily concentrated in energy loans.

Again, as institutions faltered, I volunteered for some of the most difficult examinations to gain the experience needed to grow. My willingness to step into the fire earned me a reputation as a calm, competent examiner, trusted to handle high-stakes situations. Soon, I was called on to assist with examinations beyond my region, which is where I cut my teeth as a bank examiner.

I will forever be grateful to former Comptroller of the Currency Robert L. "Bob" Clarke for his unwavering support and for trusting me with tough career-changing opportunities throughout the country. On December 26, 1989 (yes, the day after Christmas), I received a call from OCC Senior Deputy Comptroller for Bank Supervision, Stephen R. Steinbrink who shared that Bob wanted me to assemble a team of qualified examiners to conduct an unscheduled comprehensive examination of a very large banking company located in the Northeast that was interested in acquiring another large, troubled bank in that region. And with those marching orders, I assembled a team of 200 expert examiners from around the country to conduct an unprecedented examination. The technical, logistical and managerial complexities were unrivaled and the eyes of the entire prudential regulatory industry were affixed on the outcome of this examination. Unquestionably, this highly visible leadership role altered the trajectory of my career. Bob and I remain dear friends to this day and I will be forever grateful for the opportunity of a lifetime.

By 1992, as the country prepared for a new administration under President Bill Clinton, change was coming to the OCC. Eugene "Gene" Ludwig, Clinton's former college roommate and a legal mind respected throughout the industry, was appointed Comptroller of the Currency. Hugh McColl, then-CEO of Bank of America, was one of the most influential bankers of the time and provided counsel on banking matters to the transition team. Gene, already eyeing improvements to the OCC's relationship with the banking industry, proposed creating a neutral position to arbitrate disputes between banks and regulators. He disliked the word *arbitrator* but preferred the term *ombudsman* instead. Gene, a good friend of many years, later recalled to me his conversation with Hugh, saying, "I know the perfect person. He's an examiner in Texas who has the respect of the industry. He'll do what's right, even when it's hard. If needed, he'll tell bankers as well as examiners and their bosses to go to hell, but he'll do it diplomatically."

Three days after Gene's appointment as Comptroller, I received a surprising call summoning me to Washington, D.C., which was a rare request for a field manager based in Houston. Gene presented the idea of an ombudsman's office as an independent appellate body with the authority to override supervisory decisions if appealed by a bank. Because I was a civil servant, they couldn't simply appoint me. Instead, they had to formally create and post the position. I humbly but happily applied and was selected.

In August 1993, I was officially named the first Ombudsman of the OCC. This wasn't just a personal milestone; it was a historic moment. As a person of color, being chosen for this unprecedented role meant everything to me and my family. I felt the presence of my ancestors with me on that day, their strength flowing through me. It was an extraordinary honor and a rare chance to build something entirely new from the ground up. A clean slate and blank sheet of paper, so to speak. I wondered what Dr. Aboufadel would think and how proud he would be reflecting on our original plan for me to go into an entry-level position with the OCC and stay five years at most, in order to learn the banking industry. Who would've ever thought that I'd receive the honor of being appointed the first-*ever* OCC Ombudsman.

The role carried enormous responsibility. Some of the appeals I handled had multibillion-dollar implications. And yet, the weight of the work never kept me up at night. I was guided by one principle: always do the right thing. I didn't feel the pressure myself; only the pressures around me. That clarity gave me peace. I surrounded myself with brilliant people and leaned on their expertise when faced with highly technical matters. But at the end of the day, the role was about judgment. Ask the right questions, listen, and then make the best decision possible, even if it wasn't the popular one. The position gave me the opportunity to meet nearly every major banker in the country and build enduring relationships. I served as Ombudsman from 1993 until my retirement on March 3, 2008, holding final authority over all appellate matters.

After the September 11 attacks, during national emergencies, or when the Comptroller was unavailable, I was designated Acting Comptroller of the Currency. During this period, I received several honors, including the Hammer Award from Vice President Al Gore. My time as Ombudsman taught me countless lessons—but it was the journey to that role that shaped my character most. I learned to swim upstream through shark-and-piranha-infested waters, to keep calm under fire, and, most importantly, to always rise above. As the great Michelle Obama said, "When they go low, we go high." I owe a great debt of gratitude to Mae Denmond, who supported me throughout my tenure and remains a dear friend. I'm forever thankful for the three remarkable women who worked in OCC's DC Headquarters office—Barbara Jennings, Beverly "Bev" Burnette, and Ann Taylor—whose friendship and faith carried me. They had my back!

Even now, I reflect on how far I've come from the early days when I was dismissed, overlooked, or threatened simply because of the color of my skin. Once, during a bank examination near Houston, I uncovered a borrower fraudulently pledging the same herd of cows at multiple institutions. When he realized I'd caught him, he stormed into the bank, hurled the N-word at me, and threatened my life. My friend and mentor, Bob Williams, acted immediately. He contacted the U.S. Marshals, who protected me and our team throughout the remainder of the examination.

Another time, in Biloxi, Mississippi, I was invited to speak at a banking convention. That morning, after a run on the beach, I stopped by the ballroom to check the setup, and a woman preparing the room mistook me for a hotel staffer.

"There you are," she said briskly. "You were supposed to be here earlier to help me."

"I'm happy to help," I replied, puzzled, "but I'm actually the speaker."

Her face was flushed as she stammered out an apology. I reassured her and used the moment to share a lesson on assumptions and grace.

Incidents like that were not rare. I've been mistaken for a valet attendant, passed up by taxi drivers, and even had a colleague presumed to be the man in charge instead of me, simply because of the difference in our skin tones. The racism I've endured over the years both personally and professionally has been both overt and subtle, but it never defined me. I never let bitterness take root. Instead, I chose joy. I chose dignity. And I kept climbing. Today, I look back not with anger, but with immense gratitude. I'm still standing, and proud to tell my story of triumph.

***

On a typical steamy day, June 17th, 2007, to be exact, while driving home from church, Valerie and I decided it was time for me to retire from federal service with the OCC. I was eligible for retirement and felt that I had taken the role of ombudsman as far as I could. I swiftly notified the powers that be of my decision. Shortly after, I flew to Washington, D.C., to meet with John Dugan, who had taken over as the Comptroller of the Currency at the time.

Valerie and I were strategic about the timing of my retirement. At that point, Valerie worked at Shell, overseeing their offshore financials, so we timed it according to her workload, as well.

"I won't leave you high and dry," I assured John, during the conversation in which I announced my intentions to retire. "I'll even give you time to select my successor."

From there, we crafted a plan to identify my successor, aiming for my retirement around my fifty-sixth birthday in March.

Around the same time, I received a call from my long-time friend, Sam Pyland, whom I had known since 1981. Sam had worked for the FDIC before moving to the Bank of the Southwest, where he was in charge of credit administration during a challenging period in the banking industry, and served as my primary liaison during one of the largest bank examinations I led at the OCC. After leaving the bank and the tumult of the industry, Sam had a successful career with Coopers & Lybrand. Despite our busy careers, we managed to stay in touch, talking a few times each year. So, I was surprised when he called to tell me he had retired from Coopers & Lybrand and opened the first domestic office of Alvarez & Marsal outside of New York, in Houston, TX.

"I'm back in town," he exclaimed. "And working for Alvarez & Marsal now."

"What the hell is Alvarez & Marsal?" I asked, genuinely perplexed.

Little did I know at the time that this unfamiliar company would become the foundation for another fulfilling career for me. However, that's how God works...

It turns out that Sam and the founders, Tony Alvarez and Bryan Marsal, had been discussing the creation of a new financial industry practice focused on banking. They had been searching for a leader with extensive relationships in the industry and respected by the bank regulatory agencies. Sam mentioned me to them, not knowing I was transitioning from my role as the OCC Ombudsman. The timing couldn't have been more perfect.

After reconnecting, we began discussing the opportunity and meeting with other managing directors of A&M. Ironically, while they were courting me for the role, my daughter Jaclyn was interviewing with the company for an internship in a different division. This turned out to be a blessing for her, setting the trajectory for her young career. After several weeks of discussions and meetings, I had the opportunity to sit down with Tony Alvarez and Bryan Marsal, and I walked away with an employment agreement and an LLC agreement to establish a financial industry advisory service business at A&M.

On March 3, 2008, after thirty-four years of federal service, I officially retired from my position as the Ombudsman at the OCC. Just two months later, on May 1, 2008, I joined Alvarez & Marsal Holdings, LLC as a Managing Director and Founding CEO of Alvarez & Marsal Financial Industry Advisory Services, LLC. It truly felt like a match made in heaven, and once again, God's timing proved to be perfect.

HOUSTON RETIREMENT RECEPTION COMMENTS
SAM GOLDEN
THURSDAY, FEBRUARY 28, 2008
FEDERAL RESERVE BANK-HOUSTON BRANCH

THANK YOU...

To my God, for your kindness, grace, mercy, forgiveness, sense of purpose, and for giving me the most wonderful, caring, supportive, beautiful and loving woman in this world as a best friend...

Honey, this journey of thirty-three plus years would not have been possible without you. You always had the capacity to keep me grounded and insisted that I never take myself too seriously. You are my queen and are an amazing, virtuous woman of God. This journey would not have been possible without you and the unquantifiable best friend that you've been to me.

To our three incredible children who are here today (Jonathan, his lovely wife Kristen, and my adorable granddaughter Ava, as well as my uniquely special daughters, Jaclyn Denise and Janna Michelle), thanks for: your love, care, support, understanding; for the joy that you have and continue to give to me; and for the privilege of being your Dad.

To Bob Williams, my first OCC boss, thanks for the chance, the support and wise counsel, and the trust, when it was not popular, and when it was often questioned why you did what you did for someone God created to look like me.

To former Comptroller of the Currency Gene Ludwig, for the opportunity of a lifetime and for having the amazing vision and courage to establish OCC's Office of the Ombudsman, but more importantly, for being who you are, and for all that you've done to support and mentor me.

To former Comptroller Bob Clarke, if you had not trusted me to assume the leadership of key exams of multinational banking organizations during the late eighties and early nineties, I would have never been entrusted with the role of Ombudsman...I'll never be able to say thank you with enough emphasis.

Now, to most of you, those who I've had the chance to serve on the same team with, you are what make OCC such a wonderful organization. To many who I've had the pleasure of getting to know well, and some who have become true friends...thanks for the privilege.

Finally, to my dear friends and relatives...[pause]...I have no words to express all that you mean to me and always will!!!

I'm humbled by just how fortunate and blessed I've been. I'm fully aware of the unique opportunity that I've been afforded...one where I've been able to use the gifts bestowed and couple them with my heart all in an effort to serve others. I've had the privilege of working with an extraordinary group of dedicated professionals as we built OCC's Office of the Ombudsman into an organization that takes pride in serving others and in making a constructive difference for thousands of bank consumers, for hundreds of bankers, and for all of us within the OCC family. It's been a journey extraordinaire! I will never be able to communicate sufficiently how much I appreciate you.

Craig and Maria are in the room today, but many others are in Houston at their post of duty, particularly Mrs. Mae Denmond...who has been an angel for me!! Mae is an example of a person who walks a life believing what is possible versus what is not; what can be, versus what can't be; and that the efforts of one person can make a difference.

I am grateful for the presence to understand, accept, and appreciate that life is a journey that is more joyous if lived with passion, purpose and faith. I would be remiss if I did not, with deference, acknowledge the impact of those who are no longer with me, upon whose shoulders I still stand, who loved, supported, disciplined, and pushed me—my parents and grandparents.

They equipped me with the confidence to believe that the color of my skin was not an impermeable barrier or hurdle, but rather, created a mandate to prepare me for the journey. And an obligation to give the best of my heart, mind, and soul, and never to forget that selfishness would not be rewarded in the long run, while a life of service was a source of unquantifiable joy, peace and fulfillment. Those old folks were wiser than I'll ever be, and I will always be grateful for the value of that education I received at Wharton...yes... Wharton!!!

My parents and grandparents were rich in wisdom and generous in sharing all that they had. They preached, drilled, and insisted on adherence to and understanding of what living a life of stewardship really meant, as well as the impact it has on others, and that is how we should choose to use our time, talent, resources, and influence. If given to self-gratifying or aggrandizing purposes, no legacy of substance is established. Whereas if you touch, impact, and mold the lives of others, then the legacy never dies.

They gave me the willingness to Dream big, accompanied by the Courage to stay the course when the storm winds blew. In an unwavering way, they insisted on a steadfast walk of the 3D's (Desire, Discipline, and Determination) to work hard, but never without giving all of your heart, never while feeling entitled to what you had not earned, and never by having pity parties where you were the center of attention. They never let me forget that selfishness was not a part of this journey, with one huge exception, and that was in getting prepared for the race, which permits greater capacity to give more. In the words of my grandmother (and she's with me now saying, That's my boy!!), "There are smarter, and certainly wealthier, people that you will encounter along this journey of life, but no one can beat you at giving the best that God gave you. Give it all—your heart, mind and soul." Clearly, as many of you who know me know, I stand at the peak of Mount Imperfect...but I'm comforted in knowing that I've given the best that I had the capacity to give for almost thirty-four years to this organization and its people!

This journey has not been easy (and I did not expect it to be), but I can honestly say that it's been a joy, and I am humbled by the opportunities and privileges I've been afforded. In the eloquent words of Dr. Martin Luther King, Jr.: "The ultimate measure of a man is not where he stands, in moments of comfort and convenience, but where he stands at times of challenge and controversy."

OCC is a uniquely special organization because of its people and that's the only component of its composition that will impact its future successes, as well as its clients, customers and constituents. My grandmother would be pleased because God knows I've given the best effort that I could.

The storm clouds are looming on the horizon and tough times will accrue in some form or fashion that will challenge OCC's capacity and its character. Because of its people, no challenge is insurmountable as long as the foundation is solid. My challenge and my plea is that you continue to lead with your hearts. Always remembering that teams that stick together win battles and those that are internally weakened by bickering and fighting implode. It truly is all about PEOPLE!..... For those of you in positions of leadership, power and influence, extract joy from giving to others what has been given to you....A CHANCE! Diversity of gender, race, views, backgrounds, and perspectives. However one chooses to slice the pie...is good and only makes our foundation more solid. Have the courage to swim upstream and to make courageous people decision that are deserved...it's done one selection at a time.

Finally, THANKS, THANKS, AND THANKS for the opportunity. The people of OCC will always occupy a warm place in my heart and I will forever be grateful! This phase of the journey is coming to closure, but the most important element–the RELATIONSHIPS–will never end, and for that, I thank you!!

A Treasured Friendship
The Greatest Dividend
of the Financial Crisis
by Lunsford Bridges

I FIRST MET SAM in March of 2009, when I was president of Metropolitan National Bank in Little Rock, Arkansas, where I had served since 1985. In the early part of the 2000s at Metropolitan, we developed some issues related to our real estate portfolio. The regulators told us we had to do something, so needless to say, we were greatly concerned. The bank was owned by Doyle Rogers. Doyle had a real estate background and we prided ourselves on being a "family bank." His vision was to grow Metropolitan into a statewide bank, but the first big step was to have a major presence in Northwest Arkansas, which was growing rapidly at the time.

The economy in Northwest Arkansas was booming, but when the financial crisis of 2008/2009 hit the country, the real estate market hit a brick wall and Metropolitan was not exempt from this tsunami of financial turmoil. With the stress of the increased scrutiny from bank regulators, I reached out to a dear bank consultant friend, Alex Sheshunoff, for guidance, and just as quick as you can flip a switch, he said, "I've got the perfect person for you to talk to." That man was none other than Sam Golden.

Sam had retired from an illustrious thirty-four-year career at the Office of the Comptroller of the Currency (OCC), where he had served as the first OCC Ombudsman, which I thought was quite impressive and no doubt why he was recommended for the job. He had just gone to work with Alvarez & Marsal (A&M) to establish and lead their bank consulting division. Although a giant in the global consultation business, A&M did not have a financial sector at the time, so it was obvious why Sam was the man they selected for the job. I immediately called him, introduced myself, and explained our needs. He and a colleague were out of town on another project at the time, but Sam quickly obliged, saying, "We'll just change our flight to Little Rock, so we can sit down and talk."

The next day, Sam and his colleague came into the bank and met with me and Susie Smith, who was the CFO of Metropolitan and my right (and left) hand at the time. Our two-and-a-half-hour meeting with Sam was just as divine as it was informative. He exuded so much confidence and charisma that he made us feel totally comfortable, even with his stringent line of questioning. We instantaneously knew that we were talking to someone who could truly help us, and we surely needed it. If you're familiar with the world of banking, you know that when a bank gets into trouble, one of the first things that regulators, consultants, or anyone else is going to want to know is if there are any "snakes in the weeds," which is a fancy way of asking if there are any omissions or missteps that may sound alarms with bank regulators if discovered. We were very fortunate in that we had nothing to hide. The last thing we would ever have done was to mislead the one person who could help us get our *fat out of the fire*, which was Sam.

The effort that Sam put into our project over the next few years after coming onboard was simply incredible, and the roster of players he recruited to help was quite impressive. Through his thirty-four-year tenure with the OCC, Sam had built a powerhouse team of experts that he could call on for help, and that he knew could come in and turn over every stone at the bank in order to get a clear picture of where we stood.

From our perspective, it was a very scary situation to have outside people come in, but we were an open book with Sam. Through his leadership, he helped to ensure that we all communicated thoroughly and respectfully. While the review itself took place over a period of two to three months, the total effort, which was led by Sam, was a five-year process. During this time, I got to see him under every condition you can imagine, and he got to see me in the same manner.

The relationship that developed between me, Doyle, Sam, and my management team was special. As the old saying goes, *The smart person knows what to say, but the wise person knows when and if to say it.* Well, Sam was both smart and wise. His inherent ability to understand human nature allowed him to be able to analyze people pretty quickly. This, along with his multiple skillsets, helped us to reestablish credibility with the regulators who were pressing us to sell the bank. We could have never accomplished what we did without Sam or his leadership, his detail-oriented skillset, and his vast network of expert contacts.

All things considered, I would have to say that the qualities I have most admired about Sam, both during that time and in the years I've known him are, by far his loyalty, insightfulness, and persistence. Sam is the most loyal and trustworthy person I know. With him, you never have to worry about looking over your shoulder. He's also a very calm person and while he can be firm and edgy when he needs to be, I've never once seen him lose his cool, even in the most stressful of situations. Instead, he is always the calm in the midst of the storm, and anytime I've ever talked to Sam about the hardest of subjects and situations,

I've ended our conversations feeling better. Sam's strong commitments to his work, his family, his clients, and his faith are unparalleled, and among the many attributes I admire in him.

Around the time of the fiftieth anniversary of the integration of Little Rock Central High School, an event was held where the original nine Black students who were the first to integrate the all-white school back in 1957 were in town for the anniversary of that desegregation. A key member of our bank's management group, Virgil Miller, co-chaired the event, which featured former President Bill Clinton as the keynote speaker. As co-sponsors of the anniversary event, we received one of the limited-edition posters, autographed by all nine of the original Little Rock students. I recall that during one of the many trips Sam and his lovely wife, Valerie made to visit the bank and spend time with my wife Carol and me, he asked to visit the school.

We were more than happy to drive them over, and when they got out of the car to take pictures, it was quite obvious how much the experience meant to them. So, a couple of months after receiving the commemorative poster, Susie Smith and I devised a plan in which we worked with Sam's administrative assistant in Houston to make sure he received the poster, which we'd had framed, wrapped, and shipped. Susie Smith and I had a visit planned to see Sam anyway, so that the timing couldn't have been more perfect.

I'll never forget the heartfelt look on Sam's face when he unwrapped the poster. It felt so incredibly good to give something so special to someone equally as special, and who meant so much to us. The fact that in some small way we were able to reward him, other than monetarily, for all he had done for us, was just as precious as it was priceless.

All things considered, I am proud to know Sam and to have had the privilege to work alongside him and call him my friend. I have no doubt that the impact of Sam's life and this book will extend far beyond the Goldens, in terms of who will read it and the lives it will touch, much in the same manner that Sam has touched my life...

A GIANT AMONG MEN
by John Abraham

SAM AND I MET in October of 1977, at Gethsemane Missionary Baptist Church in Houston, Texas. My family had recently accepted a transfer with Standard Oil of California (Chevron) from Baton Rouge, Louisiana.

Sam and I immediately connected on a spiritual and professional level and quickly discovered that our love of God, family, friends, and the mission of the church were among the many affections that we shared. Our bond grew as we discovered our common love for the great outdoors, and for hunting in particular. We acquired our very first hunting lease in 1979 on 100 acres in Oakwood, TX, owned by a dear, sweet lady named Mrs. Kissie.

I'll never forget how Sam and I meticulously built our deer blinds and hauled them to Oakwood three weeks early, in anticipation of "opening day." I also fondly recall how on that first Saturday in November each year, we'd leave home at 3:00 a.m. in order to arrive at our hunting site by 5:15 a.m. Our pockets were often filled with pecans and other snacks of choice in preparation for long days and sometimes even longer nights, due to our time spent hunting coupled with the distance we had to travel.

Unfortunately, during our first season out, we did not get a single deer. Our second season was no different. By the third season, we chose not to renew our lease in Oakwood but instead secured a second hunting lease just outside of Huntsville, TX, where we enjoyed 1,800 acres on the Gibbs Estate. It was there that we hunted for several years, with little to no success of a good white tail harvest, so after two seasons, we decided to move on to our third hunting location, at the Cain's ranch in the Pearsall/ Uvalde area.

We typically arrived early on Thursday evenings, and on Friday nights, we enjoyed a good home-cooked meal complete with delicious desserts, courtesy of the Cain's. We fared more successfully at the Cain's and often left with plenty of spoils in the form of white-tailed deer that we took home to transform into sausage.

By the time Sam and I entered our fourth deer hunting season together, our expertise in hunting had grown exponentially, just like our friendship. During that same season, we acquired more space on the Runnels Pierce Ranch in Magnet, TX, in Matagorda County, where we shared a 1,500-acre lease on over 3,000 acres of land with a group of eight other hunters, who became friends. It was there that we enjoyed an abundance of white-tailed deer, wild hogs, doves, squirrels, raccoons, and wild turkeys, which we shared with church members, family, and friends when we returned home.

Year after year, Sam and I packed up our gear and headed to our lease. Out there in the wide-open space, amidst the still of the day and quiet of the night, the bond between us grew. I often reminisce about the times we sat around our campsite, either philosophizing about life or challenging ourselves to focus on making our own little piece of the world a better place. Ironically, enough, during our years of hunting and countless conversations, we never talked about our work, finances, or accolades, but instead shared stories of our lives as husbands, fathers, and men of God. Although not biological brothers, Sam is, without question, my brother. I have no doubt that if I needed him, he would not hesitate to respond. Over the years, we have faced many challenges together, including the survival of prostate cancer, and have been constants in the lives of our collective families.

Simply put, Sam is one of the most genuine and trustworthy individuals I've ever known and he is a true giant among men, whom I am proud to call my brother and my friend. Compassionate, humble, and well-grounded in his faith, he has and continues to make a difference in every corner of the world that he touches. I have personally witnessed Sam and his climb to greater heights, without pride or arrogance, but instead, with gratitude and humility. He is, without question, a chosen vessel. Sam is a true Christian and family man, twenty-four hours a day, seven days a week. Part of his mission in life is to help others, and the men and women in Sam's social and professional circles can attest that Sam Golden makes everyone around him better.

I remember the time when our former pastor, the late Reverend Hayward Edward Joseph Wiggins, asked Sam to give the introductory speech to the National Baptist Convention, which was held in Houston that year. Sam thought about it for a couple of days but then went back to Pastor Wiggins and respectfully declined. Sam told Pastor Wiggins that he knew an individual who was better suited, and much more deserving of the honor than he was. That individual was eight-year-old Jaynacia Lynn Abraham. Long story short, this young lady gave a tremendous introductory speech and received an astounding standing ovation. She later went on to win a National Public Speaking Contest. Sam could have easily used the opportunity and platform offered to him to showcase his skills and talents and to gain accolades for being the great public speaker he is, but he chose not to do so. Instead, he chose to inspire the next generation by blessing young Jaynacia with the opportunity.

In the financial world where Sam's name is etched in stone, I believe some of his tremendous contributions will never be known. Likewise, some of the personal experiences and incredible stories of triumph and tribulation within the ranks of the nation's top financial industries will be an experience that only he will remember and hold dear to his heart.

Although Sam, through the gifts granted to him by God, has worked alongside the financial giants of the world, it did not and has not changed him or the way he lives his life. His faith in God, his family values, and his genuine desire to help others are true characteristics that have made Sam the person we all love and treasure today. Those who know my friend know that Valerie is the love of his life, along with his children, grandchildren, and friends. What they may not know is that I proudly refer to him as a "second father" to my one and only daughter.

Mrs. Alice Williams, one of Sam's grandmothers, had a tremendous impact on him from the day that he was born. She prayed *for* and *with* him daily and helped to mold him into the great man he is by pouring wisdom, faith, and loving care into his daily life and upbringing. Through him, her legacy lives on... Sam and I often marvel at the many similarities we share, like losing our beloved mothers unexpectedly while under the age of forty. In addition, Sam and I are both prostate cancer survivors. Thanks to him, I was able to get a much-needed second opinion from a renowned specialist on my diagnosis, as well as the best course of treatment.

While I could go on and on about Sam and what a blessing he is to me and to all who he graces with his presence, I will close by saying this: when I think of Sam, I am often reminded of the 1955 classic western movie, "The Tall Men," starring Clark Gable,

Robert Ryan, Jane Russell, and Cameron Mitchell. Robert Ryan made a profound statement: *"There goes the only man that I ever respected. He is what every boy thinks he is going to be when he grows up and wishes he had been when he is an old man."* That is the Sam Golden I know.

FAMILY, FAITH & MENTORSHIP

Reflecting on my life's journey, I am filled with gratitude for the blessings God has bestowed upon me. Central to my story are my parents who raised me, their only child. Despite not having siblings, I grew up surrounded by a community of friends who felt like brothers and sisters. This supportive village played a crucial role in guiding me, and with a few minor missteps, I owe much of my character to their influence. One pivotal moment etched in my memory occurred just before I left for college.

It was a cloudy day in April of 1970, shortly after it had rained just enough to put a slight sheen on the streets of Wharton. As we typically did after school, some of my buddies and I stopped at the Dairy Mart, which was right across the street from a church about a block and a half from where I grew up on Elm Street. I was in my beloved blue 1961 Chevy Biscayne, which I paid just $195 for. In a moment of youthful exuberance, or what some might call hard-headed stupidity, I performed doughnuts in the parking lot, only to be met with a thick cloud of smoke and the sight of my mother who had been watching me the whole time. To say that I was racked with fear would be an understatement.

"Go home Sam," she said in her typical calm and cool demeanor. "I'm glad you're not dead."

Though I had worked hard to buy the car with the money I earned from mowing lawns in the neighborhood, my mother reminded me that she held the title to the car and that such behavior did not earn the privilege of ownership. She sold my beloved Biscayne, breaking my heart, but allowed me to keep the proceeds. It was just enough to buy a stereo system and some school clothes, which I was grateful for. My mother was a strict disciplinarian, driven by love and principles. I thank God for her guidance. Without her, I wouldn't be the person I am today. As I embarked upon fatherhood, I aspired to embody the same principles my mother instilled in me.

Fatherhood is a privilege, and my wife Valerie and I consider our journey as parents to be one of life's greatest blessings. Now, as grandparents to seven uniquely different grandchildren, we cherish both the privilege and responsibility. When I married my beautiful wife, I was welcomed into her loving family, where I became the seventh child to her wonderful parents, who treated me as one of their own for the entirety of their lives. Early in our relationship, we discussed our hopes for parenthood and the number of children we desired. While there were some early issues with conceiving, one of my fondest memories is the joy I felt when she told me she was pregnant with our first child, Jonathan, born just after her birthday in November 1981. The level of radiant joy I felt was unparalleled.

Jonathan grew quickly, walking at just seven months and talking very early as well. At an early age he learned quickly and wanted to know how things worked. As parents, we also quickly learned that Jonathan would try many things and ask for forgiveness later if we scolded him. He is unquestionably blessed beyond easy measure with elevated intellect and top-tier athletic abilities that millions would salivate to have. We're confident that his abundance of God-granted abilities will be used to fulfil his God ordained purpose. In the blink of an eye, three years later, we welcomed our daughter Jaclyn in August 1984, and God couldn't have orchestrated it better because now we were blessed with a boy and a girl who were both beyond precious. And Jaclyn has always been that child who has never given us any challenges. She's always been obedient and compliant and has the sweetest spirit just like my mother. And unlike Jonathan, Jaclyn almost always asked for permission before acting. Then came the surprise announcement in 1987 on our way to the beach in Galveston, Texas. Valerie announced that we were pregnant again!

Our baby girl Janna was born in May 1988. However, her birth brought challenges as Valerie faced postpartum complications, and I feared for her life. Those were some of the scariest days of my life not knowing if I was going to lose the love of my life. Yet, through our faith, we emerged stronger. Janna has the sweetest spirit and possesses a heart that is *Golden* beyond my capacity to capture sufficiently. As the youngest of our three children, she was intuitive and always observant of the consequences of the actions taken by her older brother and sister. As such, we witnessed her masterfully navigate those normally difficult and often challenging teen years with the discipline and the poise of a seasoned old soul. This because we've always been united in our faith and service to our God first and foremost, and to our children and the well-being of our family secondly. As a father, I've always not only told, but modeled to my children that their mother is first on the totem pole, because without a healthy relationship between a mother and a father, the climate and the culture of the home cannot be in harmony.

Throughout our journey, I am grateful that I prioritized our relationship, understanding that a healthy marriage creates a harmonious home. We aimed to foster an environment filled with love, respect, and reverence for God. Our children witnessed a stable home without violent arguments or instability. In addition, we raised our children to attend church every Sunday. While it was often a struggle to get three kids ready, we recognized the importance of training them in the ways of faith. Likewise, we recognized our imperfections as parents and made it a point to apologize when we fell short. This transparency reinforced our love and connection with our children. Our children often express gratitude for our sacrifices and parenting approach. We learned that true joy comes not from material possessions but from giving of your time and love. Now, as grandparents, we are blessed to pass on wisdom and love, knowing that our past challenges were not in vain.

Life is a series of storms and rest assured that as soon as you are in the middle of or coming out of one storm, there is one waiting to take its place. But the Christ that I serve is unwavering in his incredible support and assurance to help us along in this journey. Children are gifts from God, deserving of honor and respect. The greatest legacy Valerie and I will leave our children and grandchildren is not one of material wealth, but one that consists of the values we instilled in them. Our family is bound by genuine love. We enjoy being together and often see our children and grandchildren multiple times a month, which I consider a privilege and a blessing. This strong connection makes the journey of parenthood a joyous experience.

SUNSHINE
by Jomaira Santiago

I FIRST MET SAM Golden in May of 2012 at the Houston office of Alvarez & Marsal. I was interviewing for the role of Executive Assistant, to support him and several other Managing Directors in the Financial Industry Services practice. Just a few months earlier, I had relocated from New York to Houston, searching not only for a job, but for a new beginning. A new life with new opportunities and possibilities, and that would offer a clearer sense of who I wanted to become.

Growing up in the South Bronx, I had always taken pride in my academic achievements. I graduated from NYU with a degree in Spanish, yet I was still uncertain about which path to follow. That changed the day I met Sam. Something about that meeting felt different—like the sun had suddenly broken through the clouds and lit the way forward. It's hard to fully express the wave of emotion, but deep down, I knew this was the opportunity I had been waiting for. I left the interview with a rare sense of clarity and optimism.

Sam Golden was unlike anyone I had met in a professional setting. There was an immediate connection between us; a mutual understanding shaped by shared life experiences and challenges. He took the time to see me not just as an employee, but as a whole person. No one had ever done that before. He affectionately gave me the nickname "Sunshine," saying I brought light and warmth into every room I entered. But in truth, it has been Sam who has brought sunshine into my life all these years. Through his guidance, belief in me, and the bond we formed, I discovered the answer to the question that had long lingered in my heart. Because of Sam, I finally knew what I wanted to be when I grew up—a leader.

Sam has always been an extraordinary leader. He has also served as a mentor whose lasting impact has transformed my life and career. For seven years, I had the honor of working closely with him, continually aspiring to mirror his distinctive leadership style. His approach was infused with Southern charm, genuine care, fairness, empathy, and compassion; balanced perfectly with the firmness needed to convey a powerful message. Even when delivering the most challenging feedback, Sam did so with an artful combination of conviction and sensitivity. He consistently stood up for what he believed was right, inspiring me to do the same. I vividly recall him saying, "Sunshine, no one but you will always be your biggest advocate... Always stand up for what you believe is right."

From the moment I began supporting Sam, I was determined to excel in every task to add maximum value to his practice. Roughly a year and a half into my role, I gathered the courage to step into his office and propose that I could contribute in more impactful ways. Sam welcomed my ideas with open arms, inviting me to write them down to enhance the practice. He even suggested that HR review and grade a new role that would better harness my career potential. That conversation marked the beginning of my journey toward writing my own future, one that HR later formalized as the "Operations Coordinator" role.

Under Sam's continuous mentorship, as I presented additional ideas and assumed greater responsibilities, this role evolved into "Operations Manager."

Sam's mentorship extended far beyond professional development; it nurtured my personal growth as well. With every lesson, I transformed into a stronger, more confident woman and leader. Sam often shared insights from his own leadership coach and offered candid guidance on handling difficult situations. He believed in my abilities, empowering me to push forward and never give up. His inclusive approach not only uplifted me, but he also supported our summer interns, junior staff, and even our office cleaning team. His influence reached far beyond his immediate circle, touching countless lives in ways he might never have fully realized.

In the summer of 2019, following a reorganization at Alvarez & Marsal, I transitioned into PEPI (Private Equity Performance Improvement), a different business practice within the firm. I credit much of that opportunity to Sam's sponsorship, which helped me navigate the challenges of change and continue to evolve professionally. At PEPI, I built strong relationships with other leaders and found further mentorship opportunities. This new environment provided training, coaching on leadership and communication, and an expansive runway for growth. With the continued professional development support, I eventually transitioned into the role of Operations Director, with a continued focus now on growing into the Senior Director role. Even six years after moving to PEPI, Sam's presence continues to guide and inspire me. His influence has shaped the business professional—and the person—I have become today.

In gratitude for his unwavering support, I have channeled my energy into helping others find their path. I have engaged intentionally with our Executive Assistant team through mentorship and sponsorship, co-authored the PEPI Executive Assistant

Performance Competency Model, supported admin team promotions, and offered ongoing coaching during their transitions. Recently, I had the privilege of launching an Executive Assistant Community Group's inaugural Fireside Chat Series across the firm, sharing my journey and affirming that with intention, our individual paths become clear.

Every step we take outlines our unique roadmap, but sometimes all it takes is someone who believes in us to open a door. I will always thank Sam for opening that door and giving me a chance. From that moment in 2012, his light—his "human sunshine"—has shined through even my darkest of days. His unwavering spirit as a fighter, an advocate, and a champion for what is right continues to inspire me to stand tall and keep moving forward, no matter the challenge.

BEYOND MENTORSHIP

by Kelleyton J. Wilson, Sr.

IF THERE IS ONE principle I firmly uphold, it is the sovereignty of God and His intentional orchestration of all events in our lives, including the difficult and tragic moments. I reject notions of happenstance or coincidence; instead, I believe that walking by faith illuminates our paths and actions.

Believer, humble, loyal, compassionate, steadfast, and giving are just a few words that depict the attributes of Sam Golden. The bond between Sam and me, which endures to this day, is rooted in our shared faith. We first met around fifteen years ago, during the University of North Texas (UNT) Homecoming—a time when alumni, particularly our Kappa Alpha Psi Fraternity brothers, gather annually for various activities, including our beloved "Khicken on the Kutz" luncheon and fraternity business meeting. At this event, Sam and I exchanged greetings and engaged in conversation, discovering commonalities that ranged from our love for family to our passion for giving. What began as a simple chat blossomed into a profound friendship, kinship, and love that has withstood the test of time, evolving into a bond akin to that of a father and son.

While Sam serves as a friend and mentor to many, these labels barely scratch the surface of our connection. Initially, our relationship was defined by the roles of mentor and mentee, but it has since transcended those boundaries, allowing me to reach out to Sam for anything, knowing he will always be there for me. As a believer, I only look to Christ as someone I want to emulate. However, there are two men that I have had the privilege of watching model Christ by the way they live their lives. First and foremost is my grandfather, Perry Wilson, whom I can only aspire to be as revered as he is by everyone. The second man is Sam Golden.

While admired by all for his business acumen and benevolent spirit, what I admire most is the way Sam loves his wife and family. To witness someone achieve much more earthly success than many others could ever dream of, and yet never lose perspective of what matters most, is a rare feat in today's world. Hearing Sam dote about Valerie, his children, and grandchildren is enough to make me aspire to have a marriage and family unit similar in nature someday. I can attest firsthand that none of it is an act. The love Sam has for those closest to him is genuine. To know that I occupy a small place in that circle is humbling. Ephesians 1:11 says, "In him we were also chosen, having been predestined according to the plan of him who works out everything in conformity with the purpose of his will." I am a firm believer that the fostering of the relationship between Sam and me was truly God's will.

I had the privilege of working alongside Sam for several years at Alvarez & Marsal, attending engagements across the country, and it has been an extraordinary journey. I vividly remember when Sam received the UNT Distinguished Alumni Award, one of the university's highest honors. He embodies the attributes associated with this award, and much of my engagement with and contributions to the university have been inspired by his example. Witnessing the good work he has done for UNT and in philanthropy has motivated me to become more involved. Sam's spirit of generosity is truly admirable, inspiring me to plant seeds for future generations, understanding that my contributions may never directly impact me. Sam taught me that every endeavor—whether it's a business venture, a board role, or a donation—is ultimately about the legacy I leave and the lives I touch, even if I never meet them.

Sam's humility is striking. Despite his prestige and experience, he treats everyone with equal dignity and respect, regardless of their status. My relationship with Sam is enriched by the insights I've gained from observing him in various contexts: as a business leader, a brother, a board member, a family man, and as part of his extended family. No matter the role, he remains consistently himself. Witnessing this has liberated me, showing me that I can embrace my true self while achieving success.

Many lessons and qualities Sam has instilled in me have come through osmosis and by observing how he navigates life. A person who maintains character consistency, whether in family or business, serves as an inspiring benchmark. The impact Sam has had on my life and the lives of countless others is immeasurable. He truly is a giant among men, and I consider myself incredibly fortunate to have such a meaningful relationship with him. Without a doubt, he is one of those once-in-a-lifetime individuals, and I am deeply grateful for the time and access I have been afforded.

THE POWER OF DITTY THROUGH THE PRESENCE OF DAD

by Jaclyn Golden Malone

FROM MY EARLIEST MEMORIES, one name has followed me like a familiar song: Ditty. The nickname of my grandmother, my dad's mom, who passed away before I was born. "You look just like Ditty," they'd say. "You walk just like her. You remind me so much of Ditty."

Although we never met, I've always felt connected to her. Whenever her name was mentioned, it was wrapped in warmth and affection. The stories, the comparisons, even the way people say her name, make me lift my head a little higher whenever it's linked to mine.

Through the stories passed down, I've come to know her as a strong Christian woman who loved her family and had a deep passion for teaching. Seeing those same qualities in my dad, I'm convinced she played a profound role in shaping the man he became. There are so many descriptive words I could apply to my dad: loving, caring, compassionate, responsible, loyal, trustworthy, present, consistent, and strong. When you wrap all these into one concept, they equal security. My dad makes me feel secure. I know, without fail, my dad is going to show up... Every. Single. Day. Every game, every event, every concert, every tournament, every celebration, he was always there. Cheering, rooting, *fussing*, and encouraging. Filling me with the crazy idea that I was capable of greatness.

It's funny, I know my dad traveled for work because he was a bank examiner, but I never remember him being gone. Even though he was sometimes physically away, the impact of his presence was so powerful that it is the only thing I remember. Now that I am older, I see the beauty of the day in and day out. His fathering didn't waver with the changing of time, season, nor the stresses of life. Dad's presence provided a security blanket that gave me a sure footing.

In addition to being an amazing father, I had the privilege to watch firsthand a man faithfully love his wife my entire life. My dad often says, "Love is an action word," and his life exemplifies that belief. Through his actions, he showed me what to look for in a husband. He didn't have to tell me in words, because he showed me. Present, available, forgiving, faithful, expressive, and most importantly, a lover of God and people. With this "husband must-have" checklist, I was blessed to meet and marry Jermon Malone. On June 4, 2011, when my dad walked me down the aisle, there was a sense of quiet confidence in his eyes. He knew that I was marrying someone who would love, honor, and cherish me just as he had done for my mom. My dad didn't just walk me down the aisle to follow tradition. When he put my hand in Jermon's hand, he was entrusting me to the care of a man who embodied the same values and principles that he adhered to.

Jermon and I are blessed to have two children, Joah and Joy. They love Paw Paw, and Paw Paw loves them. They enjoy reading stories, attending dance recitals, soccer games, and just spending time together. As Jermon and I began our journey together and eventually started to entertain the idea of having children, I realized I had a deep desire for my kids to have the joy of knowing my dad, creating memories that would be cherished for generations to come. While I felt a connection to Ditty through stories and people reminding me of our likeness, I did not want to tell my kids about my dad, but instead wanted them to know him and develop their own relationships with him.

When my son was born and my dad held him, I just sat and cried. The Lord not only answered my prayer to have children, but He also allowed my child to meet my dad. Everything had come full circle. As a mother, I clearly see the beauty and joy in witnessing your children mirror the qualities of their grandparents. Just as I am like Ditty in many ways, my kids are like my dad. My son is a lover of God and people, kind-hearted, and emotionally intelligent. My daughter is confident, loves to pray, and knows how to captivate a crowd while giving a speech—all Sam Golden-like qualities.

I often think about the legacy my dad is passing down. One of the biggest lessons he has taught me is to live with an open hand. My dad freely gives to others. Yes, in the form of finances, but what stands out the most is the giving of his most precious resources, his time and talent. He takes his time when he talks to others, making them feel like they are the only person in the room. Freely sharing his life, experiences, and nuggets he has learned along the way. These are the attributes I want to pass down, the same qualities that were passed down to him.

When I take time to reflect on my dad's words, "We stand on the shoulders of giants," I'm reminded of the strength and love that flows through our family. It is a continuous passing of the baton from one generation to the next, intricately shaping our family's story. As I run my leg of the race with the baton that has been entrusted to me, I am eternally grateful for the sturdy foundation my dad built. And now, as I watch my children grow and flourish, I can't help but sense Ditty's presence in their lives, orchestrating a melody of connection that echoes through our *Golden* generations.

GROWING UP GOLDEN

by Jonathan Golden

GROWING UP A *GOLDEN* has been one of the many blessings that I have been afforded in my forty-something years of life. In fact, my family name is the gift that keeps on giving because as my father's "only begotten son," I have the privilege of passing down the Golden name to my son and on through his bloodline. Fortunately for me and my sisters, nurturing is synonymous with the name in that my father lives the way he loves—unconditionally and abundantly. The same love he gives to his family is the same love that was shown to him by his mother and his mother's mother and generations of men and women in our family who I will never have the privilege to meet, but who have left a lasting impression on my soul. Love is an action word and without question, I never for one minute have ever doubted how my dad feels about me.

The year was 2003. I was a rising football star in my junior year at Baylor University in Waco, TX. As a privileged, young football player at one of the highest-ranked universities in the nation, you'd think I wouldn't have a care in the world, but

I did. In fact, my burden was heavy. That year, I recall, was painstakingly tough for me as I tried to balance a full course-load, football, and the struggles of life as a young Black man at a predominately white university. Somehow, I think my dad sensed my struggle, because through the years, despite our distance or how much he traveled or the long hours he worked, we always had an inherent connection that only a father and his only son could share.

What On Earth Am I Here For? That was the question posed by Rick Warren in his New York Times Bestselling Book, "The Purpose Driven Life," and one that my dad challenged my room-mate and me to ponder that year. Without fail, and despite our dueling schedules, every night for several weeks, Dad took the time to call me and my roommate, Matt Johnson, and read a chapter out of the book. Afterwards, he'd challenge us to recall what he read and to put the concepts into action. I can honestly say that having his encouragement was confirmation that my seemingly aimless life *did*, in fact, have purpose. No matter how unmotivated and all over the place I felt at the time, the antici-pation of Dad's nightly phone call helped me to stay the course that year. That same encouragement has been a guiding light and kept me through my life's journey, thus far.

Whether it was a sporting event, a school recital, or a parent-teacher conference, Dad made every effort to be there, even if it meant taking an early morning or a late-night flight to get home to us. As the only boy in the family, I had the privilege of getting to spend extra time with him doing all of the "boy stuff" that my sisters didn't get to do like hunting, fishing, using drills and saws, and working with my hands. Those things I didn't appreciate much then, but certainly do now. And I emulate the same nurturing traits by making it a point to show up for my kids and spend quality time with them any chance I get. Being present means everything to my Dad, which is likely why, as children, we remember him being present more than we remember him being absent...

My father always talks about the fact that "to whom much is given, much is expected." I can honestly say that despite the weight that the privilege of *growing up Golden* can sometimes carry the blessing far outweighs the pressure. I feel truly blessed to be part of the family and the legacy that I was born into. What a blessing it is to have friends and people who love me because they know and love my Dad. How cool is that? I am forever grateful to him for being the man of God, the husband and especially the father that he is. I am also grateful to him for teaching me and molding me into the man and the father that I am today.

Count It All Joy

by Janna Golden Reed

WHEN IT COMES TO being blessed with the greatest parents on earth, my siblings and I can most certainly say that we hit the "parent jackpot." I am especially grateful and proud to have a father who sets the bar and the *Golden* standard in just about every area of life, from education to sports, and even marriage.

For as long as I can remember, Dad has always been my biggest cheerleader, even when I didn't necessarily want him to be. He is the one person I credit with turning my tumultuous relationship with golf, as a teenager, into a lifelong love affair. I can clearly recall, as if it were yesterday, how he dragged me out of bed nearly every Saturday morning for his weekly 7:00 a.m. tee-time with his golfing buddies. I remember him saying, "Janna, you are not dedicated if you don't get out of bed." It was my senior year during the late spring—a time when I put in a lot more practice in an effort to make it to the Texas 5A State tournament. My mind's eye can vividly picture me rolling out of the bed, because I knew HE WAS RIGHT. The extra sleep I wanted would not get me where I *wanted and needed* to be in the few weeks that followed.

But guess what? A funny thing happened along the way. The more I played, the better I became, and the more I looked forward to Saturday mornings. Eventually, those 6:00 a.m. wake-up calls became less strenuous. I suddenly started to enjoy the game that I previously despised, and as I perfected my skills, it became fun, particularly when I started beating Dad and his buddies. Outdriving them off the tee box became one of my favorite memories.

The persistence on both our parts eventually paid off and led to me and my sister, Jaclyn, receiving golf scholarships to the University of North Texas (Denton, TX) and later to the establishment of the Samuel P. Golden Collegiate Invitational Women's Golf Tournament in our family's honor, as well as hitting bays bearing mine and Jaclyn's names.

No matter which one of us you ask, our collective memory of our Dad always being present will never vacillate. Despite the countless hours and sweat equity his career required, he always made time for his family. Dad was there at every sporting event, school recital, and important milestone in our lives, no matter how many oceans he had to cross in order to get there. He's the same way now when it comes to his grandchildren.

I recall many times when we were afforded the privilege to travel with him for work. The trip that sticks out in my mind is our trip to Arizona when I heard my Dad publicly speak for the first time. I was sixteen years old. People kept coming up to tell me how much they enjoyed hearing him speak, and how they just loved my Dad. I was too young to appreciate it at the time, because to me, he was just *Dad.* In fact, the only thing I could relate to was loving him just as much as they did. It wasn't until I became an adult that I fully understood my father's influence and his impact on the countless lives of people I'll never have the opportunity to meet. The light that shines within him causes strangers to be instantly drawn, and what I appreciate the most about Dad is that there is nothing pretentious or judgmental about him. What you see is what you truly get.

I remember when I got pregnant with my first and oldest child, Maxwell, and having to tell him that I was pregnant. Although Stephen and I were engaged to be married, the situation wasn't ideal and the weight of having to share the news with him and my Mom weighed heavily on me. Lo and behold, Dad's reaction was the total opposite of what I imagined. He was over-the-moon excited, as he flashed that famous smile of his, grabbed me and hugged me tight.

Uttering the words, "Dad, I am pregnant," came out with some fear, but that feeling did not last for long...

"Count it all joy," he said, as he looked at me with his eyes full of tears.

"What do you mean?"

"You're having your first child, sweetheart. Do you know what a blessing that is?"

I often wonder how he does it... How does my Dad manage to always be that calm voice in the midst of chaos, and the soothing light that warms the soul? But I know that he inherently is who he is because God created him to be that way. And when I think about my father's legacy and what people will remember most about him when he's no longer with us, I know that we will all, no doubt, relish in the memory of how he gives so selflessly and how he exemplifies the true meaning of friendship. Whether it's the decades-long friendships he's had with my Uncle Bernie and Uncle John, or the special relationship he had with one of his closest friends, now deceased, Mr. Milton Scott.

Mr. Scott was an imposing figure—he stood about 6 feet 4 inches, was very fit, and extremely kind and philanthropic, as I am told. Dad met him in 2014 through a mutual friend he attended UNT with. I guess they took a liking to each other because they became fast friends after a trip where my parents spent time with Mr. Scott and his wife. Dad stood in the gap for him when he was diagnosed in 2019 with pancreatic cancer. Without hesitation and without being asked, Dad rearranged his schedule to ensure that he took Mr. Scott to his treatments. At the time, I remember thinking how nice, yet abnormal, that gesture was, but that's just the kind of person and friend that God created him to be. Needless to say, Dad was devastated when he passed away on December 8th, that same year.

Being a true friend, a dedicated family man, a gladiator at work, loving the Lord, and being yourself through and through are all parts of my dad that I pray I take a small percentage of. He is an anomaly. I have not met anyone to this day who is able to balance every part of their life and give people undivided attention, but this is just who God made him to be, thankfully for us.

Epilogue

IN CLOSING, I WANT to express my profound gratitude to God for His amazing grace, mercy, protection, and special favor.

Thank You GOD for your Amazing Grace, Mercy, Protection, and unbelievably Special Favor. It's been a life journey filled with diverse and varied growth opportunities. Without hesitation, my greatest blessing is knowing YOU and having the JOY of being a Saved Child of The KING. I'm beyond grateful to have lived to a point where YOU have revealed YOUR Purpose for me on planet Earth. It unquestionably is a journey that's been All about People. It's been infused by a commitment to satisfy your stewardship mandate. I know that I'm Your servant first, in all phases of my life. Giving the best of what YOU gave me has not been an ignorable obligation.

Understanding the value of the Time, Talent, Resources, and Influence given has enlightened the JOY of each day. While joyous, it's been, at times, riddled with hurdles, obstacles, and pitfalls. I can declare that my Good Days far outnumber those days of challenge. Doing so in a selfless, unselfish manner was drilled into my core by parents and grandparents who loved me to excess. Their daily sacrifices were boundless. They gave the best they had to give, including providing an environment where their discipline was appropriate, consistent, love-infused, and effective. I needed it, and recognize more now, just how blessed I am to have been reared in a family where LOVE was an action verb and practiced daily.

It is impossible to sufficiently capture in words just how grateful I am to have been granted this opportunity to live such a holistically blessed life. Having been born in the small rural Texas town of Wharton, I grew up in a racially segregated environment. I attended a church whose membership consisted of 100% Black congregants. I attended public schools for the first eight grades with girls and boys who were all Black, and with loving teachers who were also all Black. Our home was located in a neighborhood that was predominantly occupied by African American residents, with a few Mexican American families sprinkled in.

My mom was requested to be one of the first Black teachers to migrate from the All-Black Wharton public school to teach the third grade at the to-be-integrated elementary school located on Alabama Road, and willingly accepted the opportunity in the fall of 1966. I decided that I was going to remain a student at the segregated Wharton Training High School located on the west side of Wharton. My father learned of my choice and made a statement that will resonate with me forever: "Boy, there are two male figures that reside in this house; only one of them is a man...you figure out which of us fits that description." I simply said, "Yes Sir, I'm attending Wharton High School this year."

That choice opened up my eyes to see a dimension of life that is an absolute: *God creates all men and women to be uniquely special—all creeds, colors, races, ethnicities, and genders are His children and equal in his eyesight.* My choice ultimately afforded me the opportunity to see and experience what my parents, grandparents and many in my community had been telling me was unquestionably true—that I could compete effectively with anyone as long as I expended the commitment, sacrifice, effort and hard work. My experience at Wharton High School brought new friends into my life; some of my dearest friendships today originated during this period of my life. It was also a period that linked me to Eddie Joseph.

Coach Joseph was the Head Football Coach and Athletic Director for Wharton Independent School District. What started on the first day of my sophomore year when I walked on the campus of Wharton High School lasted for the remainder of his life. He loved me and tangibly made time to mentor, sponsor, discipline, and coach me. His wise counsel still resonates loudly with me. I will be forever grateful to God for the privilege of having Coach Eddie Joseph's hand in my life!

My decision to attend North Texas (now the University of North Texas) as my university of choice was again, principally driven by the time spent with me by Dr. Nabil Aboufadel during my campus recruiting visit in March of 1970. Playing Division I intercollegiate football while majoring in Banking and Finance was in no way easy, but Dr. Aboufadel often said that the discipline and sacrifice required to do well while in college would pay dividends for the remainder of my life. I fully recognize that having him in my life was not luck or happenstance, but God's Amazing Grace! While at North Texas, and done without my parents' knowledge or Dr. Aboufadel's support, I was granted the life-impacting opportunity to become a member of the charter line of the newly established Kappa Alpha Psi Fraternity, Inc. chapter. Just recently, I was awarded a white blazer signifying fifty years of service; it was a moment I will treasure for my remaining days. Being a NUPE has been a humbling experience.

While at North Texas, I was afforded the unique opportunity to serve on the Committee (along with several Regents and

Deans) to select the new Head Football Coach in 1973. That special privilege was the catalyst for the life-changing relationship I established with Hayden Fry. Coach Fry, like my high school coach, Eddie Joseph, had an immeasurable positive impact on the remainder of my life. I'll never be able to sufficiently express my gratitude for both of their investments in me.

I cannot say enough about Dr. Aboufadel, and it is my earnest prayer that somehow God will reconnect me with him or his family so I can express my sincere gratitude for how he shaped my life. As I prepared to graduate from college in May of 1974, Dr. Aboufadel's sound advice and guidance led me to an unquantifiable and joyous thirty-four years with the OCC. It was life-changing in ways that are far too many to list. Most importantly, I established some precious lifelong friendships and relationships that remain active today.

The exposure I received during the toughest of economic and market conditions created life-changing growth opportunities to develop critical problem-solving skills, abilities, and courage. More importantly, it afforded me the chance to learn that there is no difference between one's professional and personal journey... it is all impacted by your interactions with PEOPLE. I cannot express with enough emphasis my extreme pleasure in knowing that I did not practice the dangerous game of making someone else look small so I could look big. This was, and remains, one of my principal core values—a *Golden Rule,* if you will.

Now, to my most vital asset—my FAMILY. I know that God blessed me with the most phenomenal Virtuous Woman that He custom-tailored just for me. Valerie is my Queen, and—next to my faith, service, and Godly worship—is the most important component in my life. She is my comrade, counselor, prayer partner, mother of our children, confidant, and Best FRIEND. She is a strong, caring, loving, compassionate Woman of God.

We are blessed to have three truly special children in Jonathan, Jaclyn, and Janna. They are each uniquely created, yet all have hearts of gold, and I cherish the bond of love I have with each of them. I know that I'm blessed to reside in the same geographic area that affords me the chance to see them in person often. I will always be grateful to God for each of them and can't thank them enough for their unqualified love and respect.

We have also been blessed with the gift of seven phenomenal grandchildren: Ava Savoy Golden, Asher Samuel Golden, Maxwell Lawrance Reed, Joah Charles Malone, Sophia Michelle Reed, Joyce Verinda "Joy" Malone, and Jourdin William Reed. The joy they each bring to me is beyond any elevated level that I could have ever imagined.

While my parents only had one child, I do not have words that sufficiently convey just how blessed I am to have benefited daily from the love of Valerie's Mom, Dad, and Siblings. They have embraced me from the beginning as a beloved Son and Brother; I give all praises to our God!

I occasionally think about what could have been when in August of 1997, I was diagnosed with an aggressive form of prostate cancer. I must acknowledge my eternal gratitude to our dear friend Dr. Evelyn Shearer, a pulmonologist who resided next door to us, who materially aided in saving my life after I lost almost seven units of blood from an internal bleed in the spring of 2002. If not for God and His sovereignty, the opportunity to see, feel, and experience my adult children, and now grandchildren, would not have occurred.

The satisfaction of seeing our kids graduate from high school, receive undergraduate and graduate degrees, and attend their weddings, and now, to have the joy to experience the maturation of our seven grandkids, has made my latter days my better days. How could I be more blessed? The value of the time spent with my family is a treasure more valuable than anything on this side of heaven.

A great reminder of the preciousness of time granted to spend with my family occurred in June of 2025 when my seven-year-old grandson, Joah, and I spent five phenomenal days together on a trip to Washington, DC...just Paw Paw and Joah. On the first day of our trip, after checking into our hotel, we spent the afternoon touring the Smithsonian National Zoo. Joah is amazingly perceptive and analytical for only seven years of age. He brought tears of joy to my eyes when he said, "Paw Paw, aren't you seventy-three years old? I just love you! When I'm thirty-five, you will probably already be in heaven, but I'll always remember and love you. I'll always remember our DC trip...just me and you." I started the tradition of one-on-one trips to DC with each of our three children when they were between seven and eight years old, and have completed similar trips with three of our seven grandkids—Ava, Asher and now, Joah. Granny often said that **we must create memories before we become on**e.

As I prepare to close out the last quarter of my life, my heart is heavy, and my spirit is filled with alarm as our country is faced with the greatest threat to its future in my lifetime. Because the playing field is not level, coupled with continued economic disparities within minority communities, Diversity, Equity, and Inclusion efforts are needed today as much as ever. For the entirety of my life, hope in a better tomorrow for our children and grandchildren has been an integral part of my core beliefs. The climate of divisiveness and mean-spirited hatred toward people of color and women permeates the spirit of too many in our country.

While I have elevated concerns, I have, and will never give up hope that the America that became the greatest democracy on Earth will also survive this period of challenge. We always have, and as long as God remains on the throne (which He undoubtedly will), we always will.

We are better because of our diversity. The principle instilled in me by my parents and grandparents remains unchanged: *"With hard work and sacrifice, success is there for all of us to claim. For you to achieve success does not mean that I must fail or achieve less. Your success does not diminish mine."*

My deepest wish for my children, grandchildren, and future generations of Goldens is that they are granted an unbiased opportunity to sit at the table—just a chance. Given that chance, they too can achieve excellence and lead lives that positively impact those around them.

My faith has remained steadfast! To God be the Glory for all that He has done! Thank YOU GOD for the blessings you have bestowed upon me! What an incredible journey it has been! God selected me to be a FAITHFUL and KIND LEADER and not a FEARFUL Follower. He commanded me to remain steadfastly prayerful, obedient and humble to His WILL.

To the future generations of Goldens who will read this memoir, I pray that my words impart wisdom to guide you through life's challenges. May they inspire you to live a life that is pleasing to God and honors the ancestors whose shoulders you stand upon, as I have stood upon the shoulders of mine. Goldens never quit! Always Trust in God for He will never Fail You!

Most importantly, always give your best, live unselfishly and BE KIND to others.

God bless each of you,
Samuel P. Golden

Our *Golden* Family Tree

I BEGAN RESEARCHING OUR *Golden* family history in 1985. What started out as hand-drawn family trees shared at reunions quickly grew into a deeper exploration of our ancestry. My mother was raised by her grandparents, Sam and Texanna James of Matagorda, Texas, who had fourteen children. That single family tree expanded into multiple charts documenting each of their descendants.

Although our immediate family was small, I was naturally drawn to trace our lineage. As technology advanced, I began using digital tools such as U.S. census records, voter rolls, and other historical archives. Today, in 2025, a vast range of online resources has made it significantly easier to uncover and preserve our family's rich heritage.

However, tracing African American ancestry prior to 1865 presents unique challenges due to the legacy of slavery. Millions of Africans were forcibly taken from their homelands, stripped of their names, languages, and cultural identities, and enslaved in the Americas. Enslaved families were frequently separated and children were sold away from their parents and spouses were forcibly divided. Records of births, deaths, and marriages were often incomplete or maintained solely for the purpose of property ownership, not family continuity. As a result, many African Americans are unable to trace their lineage beyond a few generations.

Despite these obstacles, we have worked to preserve our heritage through oral history interviews, storytelling, religious traditions, and the careful preservation of family Bibles and names passed down through generations. While many of our elders are no longer with us, their memories live on.

To anyone undertaking this journey, I urge you to collect and protect as much family history as possible. There is immeasurable value in knowing where you come from. Your children, grandchildren, and future generations will benefit from this legacy of knowledge.

Valerie A. Golden

Samuel P Golden
Paternal Ancestry

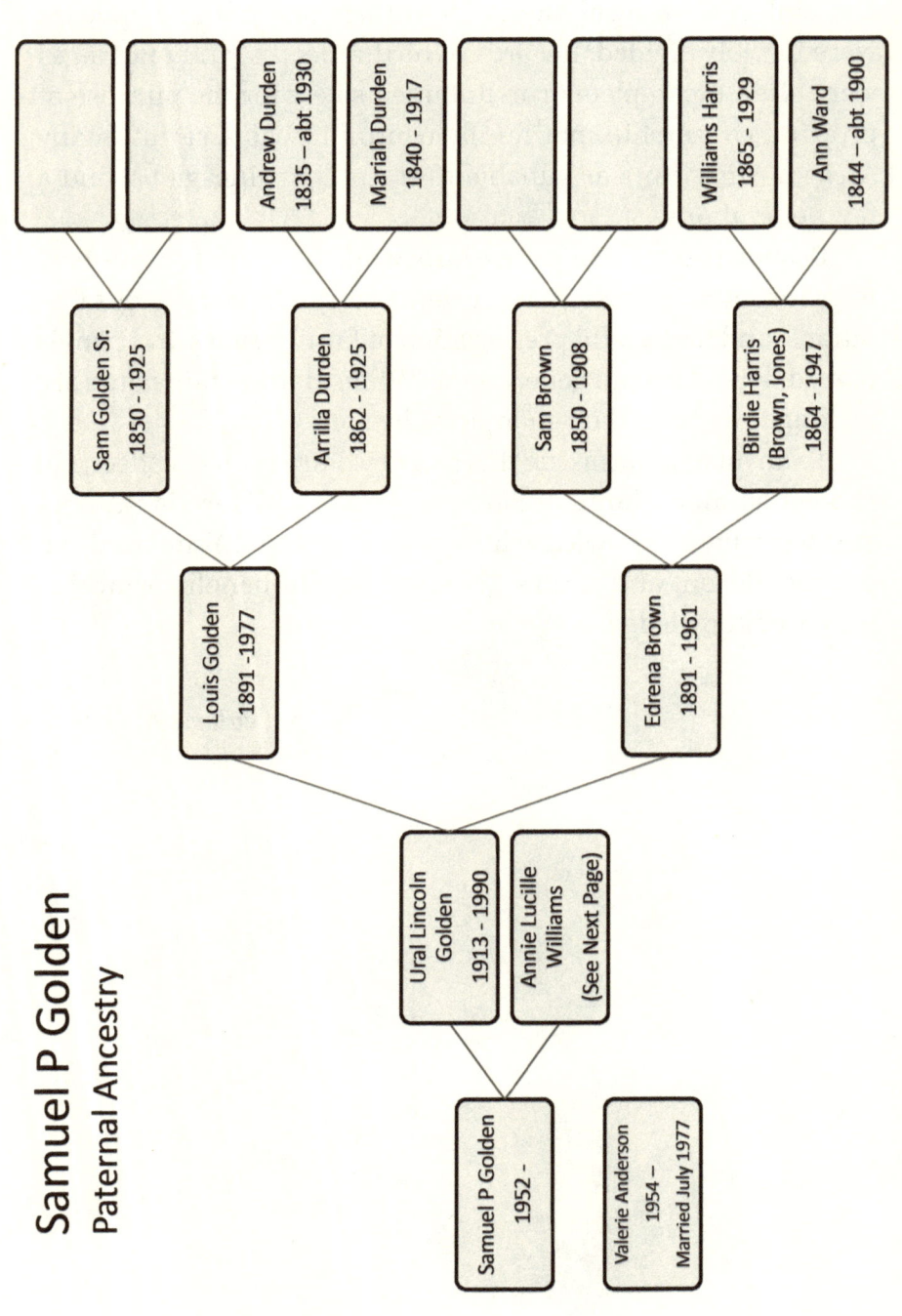

Andrew Durden
1835 – abt 1930

Mariah Durden
1840 - 1917

Williams Harris
1865 - 1929

Ann Ward
1844 – abt 1900

Sam Golden Sr.
1850 - 1925

Arrilla Durden
1862 - 1925

Sam Brown
1850 - 1908

Birdie Harris
(Brown, Jones)
1864 - 1947

Louis Golden
1891 -1977

Edrena Brown
1891 - 1961

Ural Lincoln
Golden
1913 - 1990

Annie Lucille
Williams
(See Next Page)

Samuel P Golden
1952 –

Valerie Anderson
1954 –
Married July 1977

Samuel P Golden
Maternal Ancestry

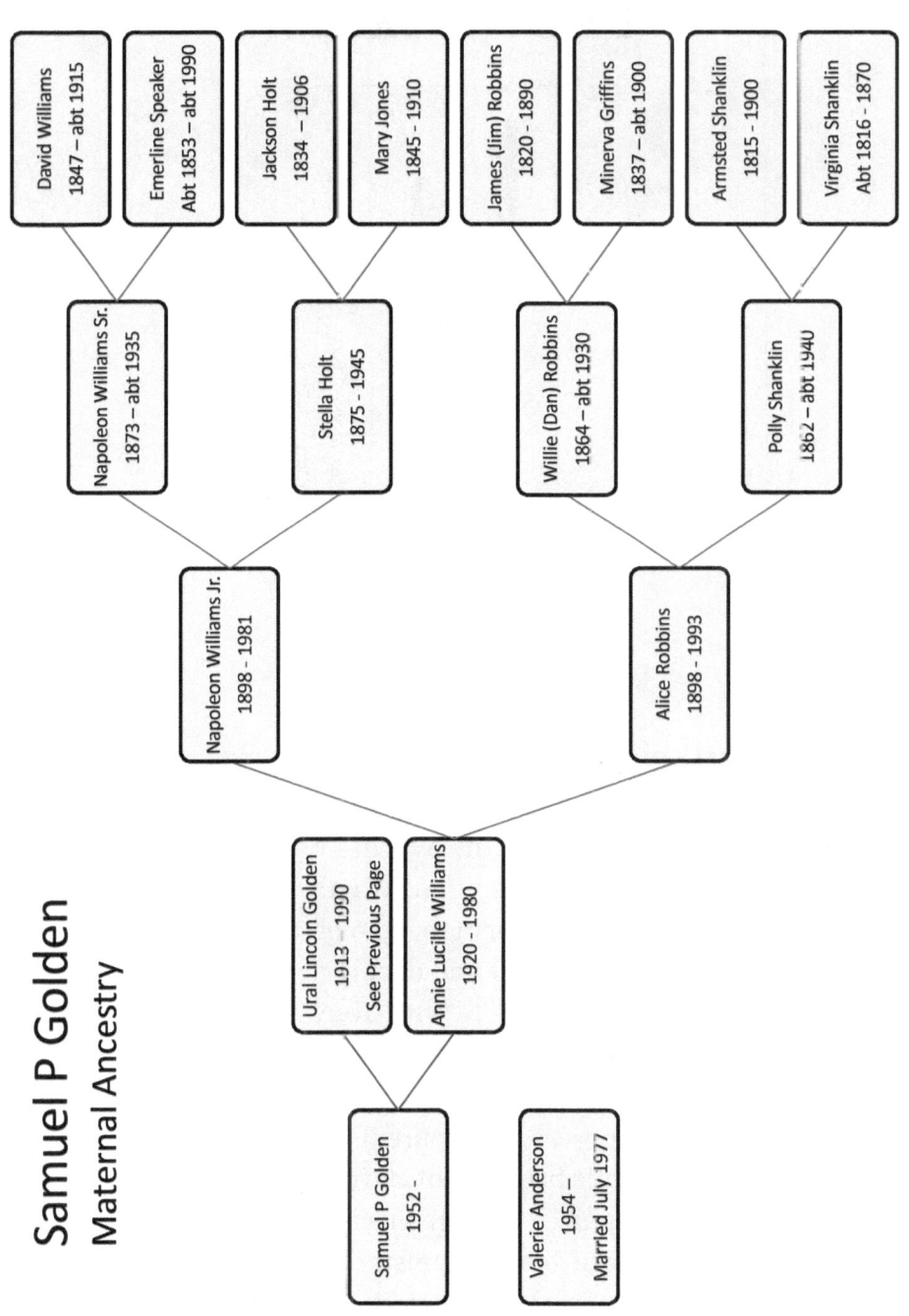

David Williams
1847 – abt 1915

Emerline Speaker
Abt 1853 – abt 1990

Jackson Holt
1834 – 1906

Mary Jones
1845 - 1910

James (Jim) Robbins
1820 - 1890

Minerva Griffins
1837 – abt 1900

Armsted Shanklin
1815 - 1900

Virginia Shanklin
Abt 1816 - 1870

Napoleon Williams Sr.
1873 – abt 1935

Stella Holt
1875 - 1945

Willie (Dan) Robbins
1864 – abt 1930

Polly Shanklin
1862 – abt 1940

Napoleon Williams Jr.
1898 - 1981

Alice Robbins
1898 - 1993

Ural Lincoln Golden
1913 – 1990
See Previous Page

Annie Lucille Williams
1920 - 1980

Samuel P Golden
1952 –

Valerie Anderson
1954 –
Married July 1977

Photo Gallery

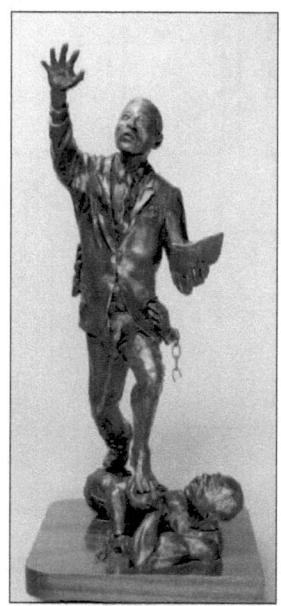

IN 2010, VALERIE AND I commissioned this bronze sculpture to honor our extraordinary family history and to celebrate the heroism, resilience, and unwavering determination of those whose shoulders we stand upon. We are deeply grateful to renowned sculptor Tony Sherman, who poured his heart and soul into creating this powerful and deeply meaningful work of art.

We spent countless hours with Tony, sharing stories of our parents, grandparents, and great-grandparents. Many of those stories are reflected in the symbolism embedded in the sculpture, beginning with our great-grandparents – individuals who, despite enduring the horrific brutality of slavery, refused to be broken.

The bronze features broken shackles, a powerful symbol of liberation. The right foot of the standing figure rests deliberately on Wharton County, Texas; a region historically known for having one of the highest concentrations of enslaved people in the state. The left foot stands upon the uplifted hands of our great-grandparents, whose courage and survival through the grace of God made our lives possible.

The book held in the figure's hand represents the enduring importance of education and our unshakable faith. Two supportive hands – one male and one female, symbolize the steady, nurturing presence of our ancestors. The figure's gaze is fixed on the horizon, with one hand reaching toward the heavens, signifying hope, purpose, and a call for future generations to carry our legacy forward.

The sculpture is mounted on African Padauk, a richly colored hardwood native to central and West Africa, further grounding the piece in our ancestral roots. We named the sculpture *No Boundaries* to reflect the limitless potential born from our heritage and the enduring strength of our family's spirit. We will forever be grateful for the immeasurable sacrifices of those who came before us.

Sam's maternal grandparents,
Napoleon and Alice Williams
(1935)

Sam's maternal grandfather,
Napoleon Williams

Sam's paternal grandfather, Louis
Golden (1972)

Sam's paternal grandmother, Edrena
Brown Golden (1955)

Sam's mother, Lucille Williams Golden (1960)

Sam's dad, Ural Lincoln Golden (1960)

Sam's parents, Ura L. and Lucille Golden (1977)

Sam's mom, Lucille Williams Golden, and his maternal grandmother, Alice Williams (1977)

Sam's dear friend and brother, John L. Abraham (1993)

Sam's graduation photo from North Texas State University (May, 1974)

Sam with his football teammates, who were also Kappa Alpha Psi Fraternity Brothers (Fall, 1972)

Sam at North Texas State
University (1972)

Wedding photo of Sam and Valerie
(July 30, 1977)

Sam and his son, Jonathan (1993)

The Golden Family on ski vacation
(1994)

Sam, his son, Jonathan, and President William Jefferson Clinton at the National Academy Foundation Institute (1999)

Sam Golden (1999)

The Golden Family (2006)

Golden Family on a cruise (2002)

Jaclyn Golden on the cover of *North Texas Women's Golf Annual Media Guide* (2006)

Baylor running back Jonathan Golden runs four yards for a score in the opening quarter, the first of Golden's school-record six touchdowns Saturday night against Samford.

Jonathan's Big 12 record game with six touchdowns scored (September, 2002)

Janna Golden on the cover of *North Texas Women's Golf Annual Media Guide* (2009)

Sam and Valerie at Sam's OCC Retirement Celebration (February, 2008)

The Golden Family (2010)

Sam with Cicely Tyson, Hallie Foote, and wife, Valerie (2012)

The Golden Family on Family Feud Television Show (2016)

The Golden Family at Sam's G. Brint Ryan College of Business Hall of Fame Induction Ceremony (2019)

Sam's dear friend, Charles Cone (God blesses you with friends for the entirety of your life journey).

The Anderson Family at Thanksgiving (2023)

Sam and Valerie in Colorado

Grand-kids at Easter in Sam and Valerie's backyard (2016)

Valerie and Jaclyn at Jermon and Jaclyn's wedding

Sam and Valerie at UNT Distinguished Alumni Awards Ceremony (2013)

Valerie at Houston Texans Football Game

Words of Wisdom

Speeches

OCC Celebrates Black History Month Comments by Samuel P. Golden February 26, 2020

"Count It ALL JOY"

Thanks so very much (to the person that introduces me), to the Comptroller and Executive Committee for being so welcoming to me and Valerie and to CARE for their most gracious invitation for me to return home. We're joined today by three special guests, Mark Nishan, Jo Ann Lucero and B. Doyle Mitchell...my dear friends, I sincerely appreciate your sacrifice to be with us.

I am touched and honored beyond my ability to express in words by this opportunity. Over the last 46 years, I have been granted hundreds of chances to address an array of audiences, but few have touched my heart like this one. This life journey is simple and truly is ALL about PEOPLE. I'll forever be grateful to this organization and its people for what it provided to me...most importantly a FAIR CHANCE to use and develop what God gave to me. This uniquely special opportunity to come HOME spawned a humbling retrospective walk back in time over the past 2 ½ months since I received the invitation to be with you today. Walk with me as a chronicle through a few parts of my journey. History is given to us as a jewel to be mined to benefit from the embedded lessons of what was done well and from what unquestionably could have been done differently. No parts of life are devoid of consequences. I'll focus on just three board categories or topics:

(1) Selected segments of my journey

(2) Why CARE and other Employee Network Groups are needed and

(3) The Mirror Test and why it's important—it's not about me!

On May 28, 1974, equipped with two Johnny Carson Double Knit suits (glad that I did not smoke because they would have ignited)....I started what would be an amazing 34-year journey with the OCC. With intention and with as much objectivity as possible, I'll now take a summarized walk through key phases of my OCC career denoting the setting and circumstances that existed at the time. I'm fortunate to have journaled for a major portion of this journey, so I had the opportunity to look back on the thoughts that touched me at the time to write about them. This walk back extracted periods of elevated JOY and unfortunately, times of utter disappointment with some of what existed at the time. I want to be unequivocally clear; I would not be here today had it not been for the 34 years that I spent as a civil servant with the OCC.

As I looked back in my journaled past, I was reminded of some painful circumstances where the color of my skin, to some, was far more important than the content of my character, my skills or my proven qualification for the job at hand. In several cases, legitimate threats of bodily harm were leveled against me strictly because I was African American if I remained a part of the examination team. Am I complaining....absolutely not. As the song that I love so much says: "My Good Days far outnumbered by Bad Days and I won't Complain." I was raised by some giants who sacrificed for more than I. My parents and grandparents would roll over if I even thought about complaining.

Those of you who know me fully appreciate that I'll never view the glass as half empty; each day that I awaken with another chance....my glass is filled to the brim with opportunity. I'm grateful and especially blessed that circumstances like what I just shared became a part of the rebar in my foundation of grit and determination coupled with an old-fashioned refusal to fail, that prepared me for the *Journey of JOY* forward. You can't appreciate where you are unless you remember where you came from!

Unquestionably, conditions today are different from an array of positive perspectives. I'll be forever grateful that I was covered for a major portion of my OCC journey by the care of several amazing white men (3 in particular) who truly cared about me as a person. Popular for them, it was not...but I would not be here today had it not been for their sponsorship. I did not make a mistake by using the word "SPONSORSHIP" versus "MENTORSHIP." In fact, with this as a backdrop, you and I would be naïve to think that the playing field has been leveled for women and people of color. I'll use the word SPONSORSHIP again later in my remarks, so please don't forget it.

This brings me to the topic of Employee Affinity Groups, also known as Employee Network Group, and why they still play a vital role as an integral part of the fabric of organizations. I'm thrilled that in addition to

CARE, OCC benefits from the efforts of six other action-focused Employee Network Groups:

Generational Crossroads
HOLA
NAPA-Network of Asian and Pacific Americans
PRIDE
TWN or The Women's Network
Veterans Employee Network

One of my greatest honors during my 34-year OCC career was the privilege to serve as the inaugural Executive Sponsor for CARE. During its pioneering years and based on my visits with Althea and Betty, the focus, efforts and actions of CARE continue to resonate a constructive message throughout OCC, but most importantly, among its membership. I must pause to express my sincerest gratitude to several key persons who, with sacrifice, paved the path forward for CARE during its infancy: Vernon Stafford, Oscar Harvey, Mattie Trice, Dian Brown and Rosalyn Anthony with constant support from Betty Washington, Glenda Cross and B.J. I'm also enormously appreciative of Toney Bland for his most impactful service as CARE's Executive Sponsor for many years.

In my opinion, the most helpful of all messages has been the steadfast and unrelenting focus on *self-help*. OCC is so fortunate to have an unusually talented and driven workforce. It's hard to believe that I've been gone from the employ of OCC for twelve short years. While the setting, circumstances and climate, in many respects, have changed for the better, much work remains on your plate. The world that we knew twenty, ten, five and even one year ago, will not be the world that will challenge us in the future. One only needs to pay a visit to classrooms in business departments at colleges and universities across our land, to quickly conclude that the face of American business will change. My unrelenting passion for Diversity, Inclusion and Equal Opportunity is multi-dimensional with the primary drivers being the absolute business need to enhance the diversity of our workforce at all levels. That's the only way we will be able to successfully satisfy the needs of our clients and constituents in the future.

Yes, it's the right thing to do and yes, it feels good.... but these factors are not our primary drivers. The OCC is not unique in that it must aggressively fill its pipeline with a qualified and diverse team of folks at all levels. Let me loop back to the issue of self-help. In my opinion, self-help does not mean doing it all alone or on an island. Again, I simply must acknowledge my eternal gratitude to three individuals (each a white man) who served as SPONSORS for me and clearly had an enormously positive impact on my professional development. I can't emphasize enough the role of sacrifice in this journey....every day was not a good day, but the good significantly outnumbered the not-so-good days. This point brings me to YOU. My dad often said to me, "Opportunity does not always knock but you better be ready if it does." He also drilled that the doors of opportunity open more for those who have a key and are willing to ask for entry. The key is preparation and preparation mandates hard work and sacrifice.

We do not reside on an island or inside a sterile bubble. Conduct a mirror test and I pray that you see part of what I see each morning. The person that we each saw first in the mirror this morning must individually shoulder primary and personal responsibility for their path forward. Never cheat yourself; others may have skills and qualifications that are superior to mine, but no-one can ever beat me doing my best. (This reminds me of the story of the GC that was building his last home prior to retiring)

Now back to the person in the mirror. That person is also someone that millions of others would trade places with and is so fortunate or blessed. On her dying bed, my 96-year-old grandmother mandated that an integral part of my PURPOSE was for that person first seen in the mirror to conduct a daily walk that would spawn positive impact in the lives of others. I challenge each of you starting with the Comptroller, EC members and Division Heads to look in the mirror. The person that you see each morning has an obligation to touch many others. It's not enough to serve as mentors...with Passion, Intention and Purpose – BE Genuine Sponsors in a way that will be difference-making in the full lives of those in need. To intentionally be redundant, I'll recap SPONSORSHIP:

Necessity for Successful Leaders to Reach Back to Assist Others

This includes those that do not look like them.

Executives should become Sponsors and Advocates of those with high potential

Leadership is a CHOICE—you consciously decide to make a difference in the lives of others. It requires guts, which spawns a willingness to shoulder acceptable and measured risks. It's my view that self-help often requires stretching and challenging oneself beyond what is familiar or comfortable. I don't espouse a belief in entitlement or that anyone owes me anything other than a chance to demonstrate my talents. You, like I was, were each hired because of your ability to uniquely contribute to the success of OCC in fulfilling its mission and objectives. I remained in the employ of OCC for 34 years because I viewed it as a wonderful place to work. I was not naïve and thought that it was a perfect environment or culture. OCC is not an inanimate organization....it is only as good as you make it. Unquestionably, it's ALL about PEOPLE and Relationships. Our life journeys would be so much richer and joy-filled if we had the ability to say three simple things and genuinely mean them:

I Love You

I'm Sorry or I Apologize

Thank You

I ask that you do some self-reflection and establish realistic goals and objectives for yourself and most importantly, do your part to successfully satisfy them. Take some calculated and planned risks, press the edges of your comfort zone, you, and OCC, will benefit.

Road Map to our Future—not for the faint of heart.

Requires unwavering commitment, passion, and willingness to challenge the status quo.

Dr. Martin Luther King said: "The ultimate measure of a man [woman] is not where he/she stands in moments of comfort and convenience, but where he/she stands at times of challenge and controversy."

OCC will not be as successful in fulfilling its future business needs without a rich mix of highly skilled and diverse employees at all levels. Easy it will not and should not be...but it will be worth the WIN-WIN RESULTS and UPCOMES. That's— MY DREAM for you!

Before I close, I must acknowledge the earthly rebar in my foundation and that's the Queen of my life who's with me today, Valerie who has supported, tolerated, and loved me for 43 years of marriage. Thank you Honey.

None of what I've professionally achieved would have been possible without you.

IT'S ALL ABOUT PEOPLE
BE A DIFFERENCE-MAKER
COMMENTS BY SAMUEL P. GOLDEN
UNT FRESHMAN FALL OF 2020

SINCE GRADUATING FROM UNT in the Spring of 1974, I have been granted hundreds of chances to address an array of audiences, but few have touched my heart like this one.

I'm imperfect but have lived a life covered by the love of family and true friends. I will forever be grateful to those upon whose shoulders I stand. Those that instilled core beliefs and more importantly, values that are foundational. I'll speak more about this a little later. But before getting too far, I want to mention and give context to one of the DO NOT's that are an integral part of my fabric—-the two dangerous words—The Double P's of Power and Privilege. My father's philosophy on Power and Intellect was brutally candid—-"If you need to tell others how important you are and how much power you have... you have NONE and if you have to announce how SMART you are, you are STUPID. I'm so blessed to have lived to a point where a substantive portion of my life's purpose has been revealed. Being all of what you can be hinges on another value learned in my early years: leading with one's HEART and giving the best that you have each day! The impact of consistency in doing one's best produces outcomes that yield dividends that are stunning because of the positive impact on others.

This life journey is a daily balancing act. This often reminds me of one of the greatest death-defying acts for which the Flying Wallendas Family is world renowned for is the TIGHTROPE WALK. They usually perform this act with NO NET and often over the most precarious landscapes, such as Niagara Falls and the Grand Canyon. Their consistent success just does not automatically happen; it requires foresight, incredible planning, adaptation to unique circumstances, precise execution and phenomenal balance. If that action does not amaze and stun the audience enough, they often step it up a level by adding a second tightrope walker. The tandem tightrope walk requires the additional skills of collaboration, careful communication, independence and interdependence and an even higher level of balance. What they achieve is no different than the outcomes that true partnership in any environment yields. As with these aerialists, healthy relationships are a balancing act...yes, there will be wobbles and a few stumbles and the occasional need to climb off and start all over again. But with shared and dedicated commitment, steadfast effort, transparent and genuine communications coupled with practice, few things can't be achieved. Like the Flying Wallendas Family...just don't look down!

The core principles of my life success are embedded in what was instilled by my parents and turbo-charged during my journey at North Texas. They've become core life drivers that govern my daily walk. Treat others daily with dignity and respect. Always remember that the journey is a marathon and not a 100 Meter Dash. Never forget that it's all about relationships: people do business with those that they like and TRUST. This journey, like all others that are worthwhile, will not be easy, but irrespective of the challenges encountered or the force of the storm winds, run this race to graduation with passion and conviction.

With reference to the mighty MEAN GREEN, I would be remiss to avoid highlighting another matter that leans heavily on my heart and likely many of your hearts. My comments are NOT political in the least. I'm 68 years old and dreamed that my children and grandchildren would never encounter some of the ugliness associated with the color of one's skin or their gender. I'm an optimist and always viewed life from a far greater than half-filled glass perspective. I attended segregated public schools for the first eight grades, purchased food from restaurants where I could not walk through the front door but had to enter through the rear kitchen door, had to sit in the balcony of movie theaters, ride in the rear of the Continental Trailways bus and use Colored Only Bathrooms. I know that things are better today (the mere fact that I'm addressing you coupled with the amazing life opportunities that I've been afforded is clear evidence of that), but **we are not where I dreamed, we would be.** In 2020 in the greatest country on earth, unfortunately, professional success, wealth and fame still don't insulate or shield you from the ugliness that still persists in various forms including racism, which is at the forefront of our minds, but also includes sexism, elitism, xenophobia and more. But know this, the culture of UNT is in YOUR hands. YOU are the future of UNT, not me. So regardless of your race, sex, or nationality you are now green and white. One thing that I do know is that the colors of Green and White, **when aligned**, produces winning outcomes just like they do on the backs of the mighty fighting UNT MEAN GREEN!!! Collaborative, coordinated, team-focused efforts not only produce winning, but it simply feel good. **A daily walk focused on decency, kindness, generosity, compassion, unity, trustworthiness, truthfulness, honesty, unselfish behavior, benevolent behavior...I'm convinced is the true American Way and those principles and values were honed right here.** (I plan to practice them for the remainder of my life!!) I do not have the words that effectively convey just how much each of you are a critical difference makers and **how much we need you.** I have full faith that our future is in great hands because of YOU. UNT is a special place and is where, despite my occasional objection, I developed and practiced many of the tools and skills that I've used in my life journey.

I challenge myself each day and if you're not fearful of the impact, I'd like you to consider doing the same. Mirror test.. Obligation to conduct a daily mirror test and to recollect the last conversation that I had with my 96-year-old grandmother before she passed: **"This journey is not about you; it's a daily test of how you can be a positive influence in the lives of others."** As I just mentioned a minute ago, focus on what can be accomplished versus what cannot be achieved.

Another saying that my grandmother often said was that **life is cumulative.** What we do today impacts consequences later in life.....each prior day tangibly impacts your ability to successfully attack the current challenges and opportunities.

I'll now get quite personal and share part of my core that drives me. This journey should never be about winning at the expense of others. It's also about appreciating that no football or basketball games are won in the first quarter but when the clock strikes zero. We must abide by the rules. Touchdowns are not scored out of bounds.

Each day will not be a good day—don't panic. Michael Jordan was cut by his tenth-grade coach, Steve Harvey and Tyler Perry slept in their cars before achieving success. Trials and tough times build muscle needed to withstand future challenges. When things get bitter, it's an opportunity for you to get better. Perseverance produces character. You have the capacity to endure because of what you've been through. You place gold in the fire to remove impurities, and we encounter challenges on this life journey that prepares us for the hurdles, obstacles and troubles that will certainly come your way.

I've always focused on three simple principles or virtues: Desire, Discipline and Determination. I believe that although life is difficult and filled with challenges, it does not have to be hard or excessively complicated unless we make it so. I'm not a wildcatter, but I firmly espouse informed and rational risk-taking. Failure to take risks permeates complacency and complacency cultivates stagnation.

Do YOUR PART, recognizing that it often involves sacrifice and self-denial. I believe in being driven by a rational desire to excel coupled by a willingness to commit to the needed effort to prepare. My parents drilled this principle into me, and then it was reinforced by coaches, who preached that "luck is preparation meeting opportunity." We are never guaranteed that opportunity will surface, but we have an obligation to be ready. Be prepared for detours. They will come. Failure is not permanent....HOPE resides at the core of my existence....my grandmother defined it as: "H"—Hold, "O"—ON, "P"—Pain—"E"—Ends. Stay in the game. Life is never navigated along a straight line. The BITTER periods in our lives make us BETTER. With that said, I get away from Bitter People because they only know how to be bitter to others. I played football while Majoring in Banking and Finance at North Texas. Why is this point relevant....for one reason....we all must be able to multi-task successfully....said another way....we must be able to keep several balls in the air at one time. At 5'10", playing offensive guard, I knew that the NFL did not want or need me!!!

I have alluded on several occasions to the basics and, in my view, the most fundamental of all principles is INTEGRITY. Your reputation and character and your good name are the most valuable assets you have. Stay grounded. There is a planet-sized difference between being **Renowned versus RESPECTED. Unquestionably, my and your most valuable asset is the heartfelt LOVE that flows out of the heart of those who love me and you— Family and FRIENDS!! Nothing is more important!! No Asset is worth more than this treasure.**

In summary—- It's not a solo; this journey truly is ALL ABOUT PEOPLE!! Thanks so very, very much for your decision to launch your MEAN GREEN JOURNEY— you clearly can be DIFFERENCE-MAKERS!! May God Bless each of you! Have a wonderfully SUCCESSFUL 2020-2021 School Year!!

THE THIRD ANNUAL CONFERENCE ON ENHANCING BLACK LEADERSHIP
APRIL 27, 2001

CONFERENCE THEME:
"Seizing Opportunity in a Fluid Economy"

SPONSORED BY

THE NATIONAL BLACK MBA ASSOCIATION (NBMBAA)

ASSOCIATION OF RICE UNIVERSITY BLACK ALUMNI (ARUBA)

THE JESSE H. JONES GRADUATE SCHOOL OF MANAGEMENT
REMARKS BY: SAMUEL P. GOLDEN
OMBUDSMAN
OFFICE OF THE COMPTROLLER OF THE CURRENCY

Thank you Tahita! I 'm overwhelmed by this, which is perhaps the most humbling of all professional invitations I've ever received to speak. Frequently, I am granted the opportunity to address large audiences of very prestigious bankers, attorneys and business leaders. Yet, never have I been afforded a chance like this to address an audience of professionals with whom I share so much. When my long-time friend, Jeff Rose, extended this invitation, I was touched and remain so beyond my ability to sufficiently express in words.

The theme of this third annual conference on **Enhancing Black Leadership** is, in my opinion, perfect and totally on target: **"Seizing Opportunity in a Fluid Economy."** Jeff asked me to take a reflective walk back in my professional journey, and I will spend just a few moments doing so simply to illustrate several points that are relevant.

For 27 years, I have shouldered a diversity of duties while working for the Office of the Comptroller of the Currency or OCC as it is often called. We are an independent and self-sufficient bureau of the U.S. Treasury Department, which means that we are not funded by an appropriation of YOUR federal tax dollars. We have the task of effectively supervising the national banking industry, which consists of approximately 2,500 national banks having combined assets of 3.5 trillion dollars. It's an industry that possesses far too few trailblazers like Jeff Rose, Reddick Edwards, Larry Hawkins, Paul Poulards and Effie Booker-Worrell, just to mention a few.

As Ombudsman, I sit on the OCC's nine-member Executive Committee and often joke that I have the good fortune of being the only one that does not reside in Washington, D.C. I'll ask your patience as I walk quickly through these 27 years of challenge, excitement, disappointment and fulfillment. I want to confess upfront that much of what I plan to share with you is not original. A substantive portion of it had its origins in the minds of a set of people upon whose shoulders I stand: my grandmother, who lacked a formal education but who clearly was one of the wisest persons I've known; my father and mother, who I thought, were tough to the point of being unreasonable, but whom I now know were simply caring because they instilled in me many of the core principles that I will now share. I'm not presumptuous enough to think that all of what I will share is ideal or that it's suited for you. It is simply my set of guiding principles, philosophies, values and beliefs. Originally they are not, but to date, they have enabled me to live a life with JOY at its center. Joy is much different from happiness because peace permeates from its core.

After finishing my undergraduate work in the spring of 1974, I began as an entry-level Assistant National Bank

Examiner assigned to the OCC's Houston office. Outfitted with two new Johnny Carson double-knit suits, I traveled throughout Southeast Texas learning from top to bottom how banks operated and why. I learned everything from bank operations to how they are funded, how loans and investments are analyzed and most importantly, how banks are managed well, and in some cases, not so well.

Throughout my career, I've been blessed with wonderful mentors (three middle-aged white men who held key senior managerial positions with OCC) who bonded with and genuinely cared about me as a person. The late seventies and early eighties in Texas banking was a period of exuberant growth where many business people, including bankers, thought that the economic cycle had been moth balled. Projections called for the price of oil to exceed $60 per barrel by 1985. At the time, I truly did not understand the breadth of opportunity that this period afforded. The turnover rate at the OCC was high, with many examiners opting to take some of the lucrative employment opportunities that existed within the banking industry. The rate of asset growth experienced by many banks was staggering, and in some cases, exceeded 40 to 50% increases each year. Loans were made to people who possessed little experience in operating businesses — in industries that they did not truly understand. It was a wild time. Many banks experienced an array of problems.

At the ripe and tender age of 29, I requested the chance to head the review of the lending function during the annual exam of Texas Commerce Bank (the predecessor of Chase Texas). TCB was one of the largest banks in the state of Texas. I fully expected to be told "no." I was not. It was an opportunity to succeed or fall on my face. It was a blast! From this assignment came the chance to not just head the exam of the lending function, but to serve as the Examiner-in-Charge of the entire bank.

At the age of 32, I was promoted to the position of field manager. I supervised the staff assigned to one of our largest operating office at the time, the one in Houston. Conditions within the banking industry in the Southwest became very difficult — so difficult that many banks simply did not survive. But from this opportunity seized, I became an expert in dealing with problem institutions, and that led to assignments throughout the country. I found myself shouldering leadership roles in the exams of some of our nation's largest and most complex banks and often most troubled institutions. It often resulted in extended periods of travel that took me away from those who are dearest to me — my family.

Despite the opportunities to shoulder assignments that placed me at the eye of turbulent storms, advancement in title and compensation were slow to come during the middle part of my career. I thank God that it did not result in me becoming sarcastic or worse yet, to lose focus. I stayed on course and through God's grace and my own determination, I eventually received the opportunity that led me to where I am today. The nation's last major recession was in the early 1990's, and it was a period where some of our largest banking companies experienced an array of financial trouble. Some bankers believed that they had few options when they disagreed with the conclusions rendered by bank examiners. The position of Ombudsman, which really functions as a binding arbitrator, was established by the OCC in 1993. I still resided in Houston and assumed that this position, like all other senior-level positions at the agency, required the person to maintain an office at our headquarters in Washington, D.C. I applied anyway, and was chosen. It was a job that placed me at the center of controversy on some of our toughest challenges. Many believed that I was unwise to take on this assignment, which placed me at the center of fierce disputes, often involving decisions that had multi-million dollar implications. That was almost eight years ago and it's a ride that I would not trade.

Now, why did I share an abbreviated snapshot of my professional career? Simply for illustrative purposes to facilitate a brief discussion of my core beliefs, values and philosophies. As a young man starting out in this organization, I established a goal way back in 1974. My goal was simple: to earn my way up the organizational ladder. I approached it one step at a time, building on a foundation of simple principles and short-term goals. It's a journey that has been traveled on a road with multiple turns and sometimes detours and stop signs. I am permanently grateful to parents who reared me in a God fearing home and carried me to church whether I wanted to go or not. I recognize that this is not the forum to espouse my religious beliefs (and I will not), but those beliefs were and remain the concrete and rebar to all that I have and will accomplish.

When I was preparing these comments, I stepped back and analyzed each stage of my career with a focus on what, how and why. My analysis highlighted distinct differences in the path that I traveled versus the journey taken by many of my white peers. I did not progress up the ladder in the same way or at the same pace. A screening process occurs in all organizations — a process whereby promising contenders for top jobs are identified and groomed early: the fast trackers. David Thomas, in his article that appears in this month's Harvard Business Review, refers to it as the two-tournament system. He espouses that in the tournament for non-minorities, contenders are sorted early on, and only those deemed most promising proceed to future competition. In contrast, the tournament for minorities includes a screening process for top jobs that typically occurs much later. This two-tournament system results in some high-potential, very qualified minorities becoming discouraged at their failure to be fast tracked early in their careers, particularly when they watch their white colleagues receive coveted assignments and promotions while appearing to only possess modest skill.

I mentioned earlier that I had three mentors at the OCC. In my career, the role of mentors has been hugely important. Despite not being on the fast track to higher-level management positions, I had influential mentors who continued to invest in me. Their investment in me materially aided in my avoidance of the most damaging trap: ratcheted-down performance or premature or early departure from the organization because of frustration with the "Good Ole Boy" system. It was a stage of my professional life where I focused most on gaining confidence, competence and credibility. I don't want to send the message that I endured this tough and disappointing middle part of my career without pain. It took much prayer and support from my best friend and personal mentor, my wife, who is in the audience today. She often jokingly tells me that she made me what I am today. In many respects, she is not far off. Her support gave me confidence to stay the course, ever sharpening my skill saw and remaining ready for the opportunity that would eventually present itself.

As I alluded to a moment ago, the role of professional mentors cannot be understated. They did facilitate key components of my journey. They often assisted in opening doors for the challenging assignments that resulted in the enhancement of my skill set where my successes (or failures) would be highly visible (challenge is not without RISK). This sent the message to the remainder of our organization that I was competent and a high performer, which helped materially in my ability to gain their confidence and to establish credibility. My mentors were honest and nakedly candid with me and provided wise counsel that kept me out of dead-end jobs — the proverbial ditch. Most importantly, my mentors willingly spoke up for me when I was unjustly attacked or stereotyped by others.

I will never forget the call from former Comptroller of the Currency Gene Ludwig, when he asked me if I was willing to accept a promotion to our organization's Executive Committee. He said two things: (1) you are ready, have earned it and will add significant value to the organization, and (2) I will not place you on an island! While Gene is no longer the Comptroller and is back in the private sector, we still maintain a rich personal relationship. What my mentors have done for me and what I'm committed to doing for others is multi-faceted and involves both coaching and counseling.

In this age where change occurs at the speed of light, the success formula remains rooted in the basics. I've always focused on three simple principles or virtues: Desire, Discipline and Determination. I believe that although life is difficult and filled with challenges, it does not have to be hard or excessively complicated unless we make it so. We make life a bit easier when we learn and understand the unwritten, but real rules of the culture within our organization. I'm not implying that you should partake in the ugly, the "cut-throat, climb on the other guy's back to get ahead" climate that exists in some organizations. But I am saying that if you don't understand the rules, which can get ugly, they will adversely impact you and occasionally consume you. Some may call this unrealistic, while others would even go as far as calling it Pollyannaish, but I never focus on failure. And I'm not a wildcatter, but I firmly espouse informed and rational risk-taking. Failure to take risks permeates complacency and complacency cultivates stagnation.

Do YOUR PART, recognizing that it often involves sacrifice and self-denial. I believe in being driven by a rational desire to excel coupled with a willingness to commit to the needed effort to prepare. My parents drilled this principle into me, and then it was reinforced by coaches, who preached that "luck is preparation meeting opportunity." We are never guaranteed that opportunity will surface, but we have an obligation to be ready. Be prepared for detours. They will come. Said another way, the Boogey Bear will cross your path—be ready for him.

I make no excuse for my uncompromising passion for equal opportunity for qualified women and minorities. I'm convinced that many senior managers just don't get it. They simply don't understand what equal opportunity means or why it's critical or worst yet, they get it but are unwilling to manage in a fashion that creates balanced opportunities for all. Please don't be dissuaded because of a lack of apparent diversity in your organization. Don't let it be a showstopper. Be prepared and stay the course. I have alluded on several occasions to the basics and, in my view, the most fundamental of all principles is INTEGRITY. Your reputation, character and your good name are the most valuable assets you have. Stay grounded. It's a small world. I have a tombstone on my desk that constantly reminds me that my greatest ability is my dependability. Mean what you say, do what you say you will, and do it when you say you're going to do it. While you have probably heard this trite saying your entire life, it's reality. Keeping your word defines you. Having a reputation of being trustworthy, honest, fair and dependable will precede you and is valued more than core technical abilities.

What some believe are the soft skill sets are, in my opinion, the basis of the foundation — your people skills. How you treat and interact with others and how you communicate with them will ultimately determine your success: Insincerity, empty rhetoric and trickery breed distrust. Never fall asleep. Stay alert, learning never stops. Remain sharp, with skills honed and relevant. This is a journey with a variable destination that is dynamic. You will always go somewhere, but you never arrive until the journey is over.

It's not a solo journey. I'm not naïve enough to believe that you or I individually can revolutionize the world, but I do know that adherence to these principles will make a difference and can influence organizational cultures. It won't happen overnight, but one step at a time. It's well worth the effort. And, when you get into a position of influence or leadership, do your part. Reach back and never forget that you stand on the broad shoulders of others who braved much more treacherous and less rewarding paths before us.

You can't be of assistance to anyone without attention to your well being. Pay attention to your health. Get regular physicals. I would not be here today if it were not for the care and diligence of my doctor, who during my annual physical four years ago did not feel comfortable with my PSA that was slightly elevated. Because of his caring and God's grace, the prostate cancer that was diagnosed was successfully removed and I can enjoy a normal life with my family. But successful treatment is not enough. I feel an obligation to help educate and spread the word to other men, particularly African American men who are impacted by this disease at a rate that is materially higher than other races. That's why you see that I am a director and President of Prostate Action, Inc. We must give back.

I've mentioned family on several occasions this morning. I value my professional responsibilities, but they are pale in comparison to the significance of my role with the other four people who share the last name of

Golden. Again, don't take your health for granted. Lastly, please use the income that you make wisely. Income does very little used irrationally but wealth permits great flexibility and I'm not just talking about being rich. Failure to discipline oneself to budget and simply say no to our desires to acquire depreciating consumer goods is the enemy of wealth accumulation.

Seizing opportunity in any economic setting is grounded in the basic! I sincerely appreciate your attention and would be delighted to take a few questions.

ACKNOWLEDGEMENTS

I STRUGGLE TO FIND words deep enough to thank my beautiful and beloved wife of forty-eight years and my best friend of fifty-three – Valerie Golden. Your unwavering love, boundless encouragement, and quiet strength have been the heartbeat behind this memoir. Through every moment of doubt, every late night, and every memory revisited, you stood beside me with patience, grace, and a calm that steadied me. You didn't just support this journey, you believed in it, even when I wasn't sure I could finish. Your faith in me gave me the courage to keep going. This memoir exists, in no small part, because of your love. And for that, I am eternally grateful.

To Angela "Angie" Ransome-Jones, there are truly no words strong enough to capture the depth of my appreciation. Your steady guidance, gentle leadership, and creativity carried this project from concept to completion. You worked hand in hand with me, offering both your skill as a writer and your heart as a friend. You are a true professional, and I thank God for blessing me with your partnership throughout this journey. To my Kappa

Alpha Psi fraternity brother and fellow UNT alumnus, Robert Mack, thank you for your wise and timely counsel. You stepped in at the eleventh hour without hesitation, and for that, we are deeply and eternally grateful.

This memoir may never have come to life were it not for the persistent and loving encouragement of our eldest daughter, Jaclyn. You gently, but firmly, insisted that I tell this story, not just for myself, but for the generations of our ancestors on whose shoulders I stand, and for the generations of our family yet to come. Your vision, along with the conviction of Valerie and our other children – Jonathan and Janna lit the path forward.

And speaking of lighting the path forward, I would be remiss if I did not give special recognition to Dr. Nabil Aboufadel, W. Robert "Bob" Williams, Edgar Q. Smith, Coach Hayden Fry, and Coach Eddie Joseph for being such guiding forces in my life. If it were not for these gentlemen seeing something special in me and taking the time to nurture that something and mold and shape it into a sense of purpose, confidence, and resilience, I might have never stepped fully into the calling placed on my life. They believed in me before I knew how to believe in myself. Through their mentorship, encouragement, and unwavering faith in my potential, they helped lay the foundation for so many of the opportunities and decisions that would follow. Their impact echoes through every chapter of this journey, and I remain forever grateful.

To our beloved children – Jonathan, Jaclyn, and Janna – and to all the beloved friends and family members who contributed your time, energy, and love to this memoir, I am forever grateful. Your voices, your memories, and your support are woven throughout these pages. Dr. Michael Sweeney, my sweet Valerie and my late cousin Estella Grant (may her soul rest in peace), Robert Taylor, Clarence "Bernie "Little, Lunsford Bridges, John Abraham, Jomaira Santiago (aka *Sunshine*), and Kelleyton

Wilson Sr., – thank you. I carry each of your contributions with deep affection and respect. As my grandmother, Alice Williams, used to say, "Love is an action word." You didn't just say it, you walked it!

I also want to thank my extended family at Alvarez & Marsal (A&M). Your generosity and support over the years have meant more than I can express. A special heartfelt thanks goes to A&M founders and CO-CEOs Bryan Marsal and Tony Alvarez, II for granting me the private-sector professional opportunity of a lifetime. I'll never be able to thank Sam Pyland enough for linking me with Bryan and Tony and for his unwavering support. I must also express my sincere gratitude to Jeffery O. Rose for his support during the early years of my A&M journey. I am deeply humbled and honored by the creation of the Golden Mentor Award, an award that bears my name and celebrates individuals within the firm who exemplify outstanding mentorship, leadership, and achievement. It is one of the greatest privileges of my life to be associated with such a meaningful recognition.

To my friends at the Office of the Comptroller of the Currency (OCC), thank you for giving me the opportunity to launch a long and rewarding career straight out of college, one that spanned more than three decades. I am deeply grateful for the chance to serve, and truly honored to have the *CARE (Coalition of African American Regulatory Employees) Member of the Year Award* named in my honor.

To my fellow board members and colleagues at the University of North Texas Foundation, it has been one of my greatest honors to serve alongside each of you. Thank you for your partnership and your trust. And to my UNT "Mean Green" family, I will forever be humbled by the incredible honor of being named a *UNT* **Distinguished Alumni** in 2013, as well as being inducted into the **UNT G. Brint Ryan College of Business Hall of Fame** in 2019.

To my brothers of Kappa Alpha Psi Fraternity, Incorporated:

and my spiritual families – Macedonia Missionary Baptist Church (my childhood church in Wharton, TX), Gethsemane Missionary Baptist Church (where we served for forty-four years), and Pilgrim Journey Missionary Baptist Church (where we now serve, just down the road from our home) – you ALL have shaped me in ways that words cannot fully express.

To the Memorial Hermann Foundation (and its Sugar Land community hospital), the Gulf Coast Medical Foundation, the Fort Bend Education Foundation, the Smith Hutson School of Banking Board of Directors (with special gratitude and in memoriam to my dear friend, James B "Jim" Bexley, Founding Chair), and the Fort Bend Children's Discovery Center – thank you for the opportunity to serve beside you and for the inspiration you've given me along the way.

Special thanks are owed to Troy Johnson of the African American Literature Book Club (AALBC); Natalie Stokes-Peters of On-Point Book Design; and to our brilliant editors – Carol Taylor, Laura Galan-Wells, and Geniece Johnson, whose insight, care, and expertise helped shape these words into something worthy of the stories behind them.

And to all those who have supported me, whether quietly in the background or with bold encouragement, you are too numerous to name but never forgotten. To God be the glory for what He has done and for linking me with a community of friends and family more extraordinary than I could ever have imagined.

www.ingramcontent.com/pod-product-compliance
Lightning Source LLC
Chambersburg PA
CBHW021149130626
46554CB00005B/1726